A FOUNDRY IN A GARDEN

A LEICESTERSHIRE STORY

Robert Charles Harrison 1874–1949.

A FOUNDRY IN A GARDEN

A LEICESTERSHIRE STORY

by

Rowles Harrison

ALAN SUTTON PUBLISHING LIMITED

First published in the United Kingdom in 1995 by
Alan Sutton Publishing Limited
Phoenix Mill · Far Thrupp · Stroud · Gloucestershire

British Library Cataloguing in Publication Data

A catalogue record for this book is available from the British Library.

ISBN 0 7509 0999 4

Consultant: Trevor Hickman
Typeset in 11/12 Palatino
Typesetting and origination by
Alan Sutton Publishing Limited
Printed in Great Britain by
Hartnolls, Bodmin, Cornwall

Dedication

I dedicate this book to my father Robert Charles Harrison whose fifty-five years' contribution to the non-ferrous foundry trade should not go unrecorded. [This and the village of my birth prompted me to write this story].

Acknowledgements

I wish to record my thanks to my wife Muriel, daughters Maureen and Julia and sons David, Robert and Brian for their help and encouragement. Without their assistance the compilation of this book would have been impossible. I also wish to thank all my friends who have provided photographs used to complement my text.

Rowles Harrison
October 1994

Contents

Chapter One   The Early Years   1

Chapter Two   The First World War and after   13

Chapter Three   Village and Family Life   21

Chapter Four   Between the two World Wars   39

Chapter Five   In the Countryside   47

Chapter Six   Keyham and Gough Road   77

The Early Years

The story that I am about to relate is centred around my father Robert Charles Harrison, born October 16th 1874, a great man and a wonderful father to my brother, my four sisters and myself. My father was the eldest of a family of four, two brothers and a sister, and they were very poor. He once told me that he was often hungry and sometimes lived on dates and lotus beans.

His father was employed as a counterman, which I understand has some connection with the hosiery trade. His grandfather was a chimney sweep known locally as 'the gentleman chimney sweep'. He employed boys to climb up chimneys and wore a top hat. He had had an education and often used to write letters for other people who could not read or write. These letters were always sealed with his own golden seal, which is now in my possession.

My father left school at the age of twelve and started work at a corn and flour merchants called Pratts in Nicholas Street, Leicester. After about two years he decided it was not for him and he would like a change. He then applied for a job in an iron foundry: Messrs S. Russell and Sons, in Bath Lane, Leicester working from 6.30am until 5.30pm with half an hour for breakfast. During his interview they remarked 'You're a fine bloke, wanting a change from a white trade to a black one'. However, he was taken on and stayed for approximately twenty-five years, until in 1911 he started his own business as a non-ferrous foundryman at Keyham.

In those days work in foundries was hard and tiring. One of his first jobs was to knock off the runner heads from moulds that were just cast and red hot. These were carried on a shovel up a ladder and tipped into the furnace to save coke. In those days the winters were often very severe and sometimes it was so cold that on a Monday morning after being closed for the weekend, the moulding sand was frozen. Some of the moulders would get together and say 'Well lads what is it to be, shall we throw the hat up'. If it came down they would all go home.

No doubt due to his skill and hard work he made good progress as a moulder. He was quick and as the years went by he turned out more than some of the others. He was rewarded by being paid more than the going rate. After a time when the others found out he admitted to them that he

Staff at S. Russell and Sons, Bath Lane, Leicester, 1889, showing Robert C. Harrison
aged 15, front row third from right.

had been getting this extra for several months, so they all went on strike.
This caused a disturbance and to overcome the difficulty and to get the
men back to work he was made foreman.

My father was an excellent swimmer and he used to teach the
apprentices at the Bede House nearby. It was said that due to his
extraordinary stamina he was able to stay in the water for hours and his
friends would say that with suitable training he would be able to swim the
English Channel.

Being the son of a Freeman, my father was sworn in as a Freeman of the
Borough of Leicester at the age of 21 years in front of the Lord Mayor of
Leicester. This entitled him to a garden or allotment on the Freemans
Common. He quickly made use of this during his free time and often he
told me he earned £1 a week with the sale of the produce.

He was a keen cyclist and his earliest cycle had solid rubber tyres. One
weekend he and his brother Fred cycled to Hook Norton, a village near
Banbury, and visited their aunts. These were the Miss Rowles, maiden
ladies. I was named after them and christened with the name Rowles. On
the return journey, a very hot day, the two brothers became very thirsty
and decided to call at a house known as the Lantern House, to ask for a
drink of water. The building was built of stone and was shaped like a

lantern, situated on the side of a wood, at the crest of a hill near Badby. The door was opened by a very attractive young lady, who lived there with her grandmother. Having quaffed the much appreciated water and thanked Gran, they resumed their journey. When outside, my father said 'Fred, I'm going to marry that girl'.

He made frequent journeys to visit the young lady at the Lantern House, on his cycle, and eventually gave her a mandolin as an engagement present. I have that instrument as a treasured possession.

As a child my mother went to school at Daventry, a four mile walk each way from the Lantern House. There were no cars or buses in those days. After leaving school at the age of 14 she was engaged as a pupil teacher at Badby School. She had a good education and this proved to be of the greatest assistance to my father when he was in business on his own. My father and mother were married in 1903 at Woodford Halse, a village about eight miles from the Lantern House. This is where my mother was born and where she lived with her parents until moving to live with her Granny at the Lantern House.

My mother's family name was Bird and her christian name was Ada Isabel; she had a sister, Cissie, and two brothers, Jack and George. Both

The Lantern House, Badby; the author's maternal great grandmother with friend, *c.* 1900.

brothers ran a local undertakers business in the village of Woodford. They were called up for active service in the First World War, George serving in the Yeomanry in Germany while Jack went to India. This meant the closing down of their undertaking business. Their sister, Cissie, carefully looked after their carpenters shop. All their tools were cleaned and oiled and put away ready for their return, and fortunately they did, safe and sound. On their return they were able to carry on their business at Woodford.

My uncle George was a wonderful craftsman and carver. Being ambidextrous, he could use each hand equally well when carving. He won a prize at the City and Guilds at the age of 21 with his apprentice piece. This carving, in oak, was always admired by me and when he died at the age of 86, it was left to me and it now hangs over the doorway in the hall of my home.

After their wedding my parents came to live in Leicester. My father had rented a terraced house in Bismark Street. What a contrast for my mother after spending most of her life at the Lantern House, a beautiful setting in completely unspoilt countryside, where she fetched water every day from the spring in the field below. My mother missed life in the countryside especially with my father being away all day at work at the foundry.

My father noticed nearby a small greengrocer's shop to let. They decided to rent this and moved in thinking it would help my mother to occupy her time. One day a very large bunch of bananas arrived and it was much too heavy for her to handle and to hang up so she asked a passer-by if he would be so kind as to hang them up on a hook in the ceiling. He duly obliged but the hook came out, and the bunch of bananas fell on him pinning him to the ground half stunned. I can remember that in most greengrocers shops in those days, it was the custom to hang bananas up in large bunches as they were grown.

During the time my father was serving his seven years apprenticeship at Russells he was trained in the foundry by Dizzy Russell. Sometimes he was asked to take the two young sons of the owner down to the market place and buy them a penny bun. Off they would go, one to each hand.

I think my father must always have had ambitions to have his own foundry and be his own boss. While working for Russells and living in Bismark Street, he hired a small underground cellar and fitted this out as a small foundry. A coke fired furnace was made and at nights after work he would mould and cast all kinds of ornamental parts such as letter boxes, iron stands, teapot stands, candlesticks, horse brasses etc. These were in yellow brass.

Late one night while melting brass, he allowed it to become too hot. It is well known by foundrymen that when this happens yellow brass gives off a dense fume, zinc oxide. This soon filled the cellars and seeped up into the room above where a dance was being held. This stopped the dance until the smoke subsided and he had to close the foundry down for the night. Nothing daunted, he carried on for some time after this in his spare time. Eventually Russells got to know what was going on. He was called up before his employers; no doubt they wondered where he was getting the metal from. He invited them down to the foundry and was able to show them all the receipts of the purchase of his metal and put their minds at ease.

I think my father realised that my mother would never be completely happy in a town and in 1905 he saw an advertisement for a house for sale in the country, known as The White House, Keyham, approximately six miles from the centre of Leicester. He immediately applied for details and soon became the owner. This delighted my mother. The house was spacious and there were two acres of land including a one acre paddock, a well-kept kitchen garden, an orchard with lots of fruit trees. The house had its own bathroom with hot water from the kitchen range. The house and land was purchased through a Building Society for the sum of £550.

My father soon had the garden in cultivation and planted some more fruit trees. (His garden on the Freeman's Common had of course to be given up as he had left the Borough of Leicester; it was transferred to his brother Fred who lived in the City.)

My father now had to cycle six miles into Leicester if he was to continue with his employment with Russells; he cycled to his work from Keyham

The White House, Keyham, *c*. 1906, showing author's mother and neighbours. It was at the rear of the White House that the foundry was established, 1911.

for a further seven years. The road was quieter then; it was gated and in places had grass growing in the centre. No one in the village had a car. There were five small farms, with no telephones, electricity or water supply.

My mother was delighted at the change. I have heard her say that these seven years were some of the happiest years of her life. She used to meet my father from work at the top of Keyham hill. In winter she could always tell his cycle lights which were always brighter than the rest. I feel sure the main reason for my father deciding to move to Keyham was for my mother's benefit.

Soon after moving to the White House, a certain lady whose family, the Rodwells, were living at Keyham Hall decided to move from Keyham. One of her daughters, a Miss Margie Rodwell, wanted to stay in the village. My father agreed to rent her the main rooms of The White House; the two downstairs front rooms and the two bedrooms leading off the top landing above, plus the bathroom. A smaller bedroom leading off the lower landing was occupied by Miss Margie's maid Fanny. She also had what was called the dairy as her living quarters. Fanny had the use of the cooking range in the kitchen which we all shared. This arrangement I am told worked quite well, although it must have had some inconveniences for my mother and father who had to use the outside toilet and do without the bathroom.

Miss Margie was Master of the local Beagles which used to meet from time to time outside The White House. My mother was a keen supporter and used to follow the hunt.

The outside pump was the only supply of drinking water we had. We were, however, lucky to have a large underground chamber which held all

A view of the church of All Saints, Keyham, *c.* 1900.

the water from the house roof – lovely soft water. This however had to be pumped up to a large tank in the bathroom. The hand pump for this was situated in the scullery. Miss Margie engaged an old man called Mandy to keep the tank full. The pumping process took about twenty minutes. Old Mandy, as he was known, was quite a character in the village and he used to walk across the fields to Thurnby on Sunday mornings to fetch the mail. My father always rewarded him with a bottle of beer on his return.

One night while cycling from work in the winter, my father got caught in a violent blizzard. This was while crossing what we knew as The Big Field (between Scraptoft and Keyham). This was unfenced on both sides in those days and was more than 100 acres in area. He got lost and strayed off the road going round in circles for about an hour. Finally he found the road again and decided to scrape his boot along the road the rest of the way to avoid becoming lost again. He ended up with the sole of his boot nearly off.

Miss Rodwell stayed at The White House for approximately two years, finally deciding to leave the village and give up the tenancy. I think my father and mother were pleased about this because the extra room would be needed for any forthcoming family.

Miss Rodwell was an accomplished pianist and had her own piano. My father and mother, living in the kitchen, were entertained by musical interludes from time to time.

The door leading from the kitchen up into the sitting room which was occupied by Miss Rodwell, was secured, no doubt for privacy reasons. A heavy curtain hung on the kitchen side where we lived and this provided a space of about 18 ins. As children we used to hide in there while playing hide and seek. It also provided a useful storage space for shoes, slippers, and all sorts of things. If anything was lost someone would say 'Have you looked in the peep'. My mother used to say, 'You are not to call it the peep'. Some years after when I was looking for something I drew the curtain aside and noticed a small hole in the door where a knot in the wood had come out. It suddenly dawned on me that perhaps this was how it had got its name.

It was during 1907 that my mother became pregnant and I was born on 28th April 1908. My father had to make arrangements for the confinement. As there was no other form of transport in the village and no telephone my father had to cycle into Leicester to contact a Dr Clark in Uppingham Road, who became our family doctor. He would get out his pony and trap and was on the scene in time. This system of communication was repeated for the rest of the family except my youngest sister Marjorie who was born in the Causeway Lane Maternity Hospital. I can remember my mother saying that having a baby in hospital, with all the care and attention, was like being in heaven compared with giving birth in a remote country village. Dr Williams of Billesdon usually attended the people of Keyham. He would arrive on horseback, or with a pony and trap with his Dalmatian dog running behind.

The author sitting on his father's knee with his brother Robert on his mother's knee, before the First World War.

My father decided that it was time to say goodbye to S. Russell and Sons and to start his own foundry. He duly tendered his resignation. Their comment was 'We'll ruin you, Harrison!'.

There were six of us all told in our family: my brother Robert was two years younger than me, my sisters Cissie, Mavis and Ethelwynne who arrived at two year intervals, and Marjorie who was born during 1921.

We all went to Keyham School from the age of five until we left school at the age of fourteen. My brother and I both started work in the foundry as soon as we left school. There was no pressure from my father; we had a completely free hand. I think, being born and living a few yards from the foundry, where we were allowed to play during weekends, we must have become addicted to foundry life.

At the rear of The White House was a building that had been used as stables. It was made of brick with a slated roof with windows on the south side, of modest size, perhaps 25 ft by 12 ft. He set to work with the help of a Mr Timson, a retired builder who lived in the village. Pits were dug in the ground and lined with high-grade fire bricks, with cast iron gratings covering them. Three pit coke fired furnaces were constructed, one of 60 lbs capacity and two 120 lb. The flues of the three furnaces were connected to an existing chimney stack at one end of the building. Benches were built under the windows and oil lamps fixed to the side walls.

The furnaces were dried out and tested, and work could start. The metal was melted in crucibles which were lifted by hand out of the furnace with special tongs. The crucible was taken in a carrying vuel to the moulds and then poured.

The first casting my father made was a bronze letter box complete with flap with his name in raised letters, R.C. Harrison Brass Founder. This was let in the coach house door facing the road on the front of the building adjacent to The White House.

The main types of castings produced in the foundry were bushes and bearings for the general engineering trade, also bronze and brass household items. Castings were also made for hosiery and boot and shoe machines, also for brewery plant steam fittings and towel rail fittings.

The largest casting made at Keyham was cast in 1921 and was a pump liner weighing 1,000 lbs. For a large casting such as this several furnaces would be required and each crucible would be charged and melted at the same time and poured into a pre-heated large ladle which would be under the one-ton pulley block gantry. In the early days of the foundry however, there were no gantries and everything was lifted by hand.

Some of the bronze and brass castings made at the Keyham foundry during the first few years of its operation.

The special foundry coke for melting non-ferrous metals came in big lumps and was ordered by the truck-load and consigned to Ingarsby Station. This was a mile and a half away from Keyham. A local carter would collect and deliver it to the foundry by horse and muck cart. It would be tipped into an open topped bunker just outside the foundry door. Being in big pieces it had to be broken into suitable size lumps to fit between the furnace wall and the crucible.

The red Mansfield moulding sand also came to Ingarsby Station. This had to be stored under cover in an open fronted shed. The water used each day in the foundry for mixing moulding sand came from the outside pump near the back door of the house. It was carried into the foundry in a watering can or buckets.

My father worked for a short time on his own, relying on local farm labourers when he wanted a lift for anything heavy. Realising that to make any progress he would need extra help, he decided to contact Mr William Lester who worked with him at S. Russell and Sons. Mr Lester, a widower and a skilled moulder, decided to come and work for my father. Lodgings were arranged for him at the farm next door. Having Mr Lester working for him, my father was to some extent free to deliver his castings, which he did in a carrier on a push bike. However this was only for a short time until he hired a horse and float from a Mr Timson, a farmer in the village.

The metal used in the foundry consisted mostly of scrap purchased from a metal merchant in Leicester who would deliver it to Keyham,

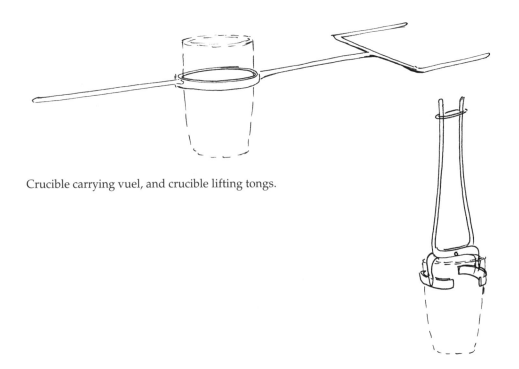

Crucible carrying vuel, and crucible lifting tongs.

perhaps in 2 ton lots at one time. My father was an expert and could pick out a suitable metal for any job. It might be gun metal for bushes and bearings, phosphor bronze for gear wheels, yellow brass for less important parts; zinc, tin and copper would be added when necessary. The copper often came from old coppers which he cut up in the yard with hammer and chisel to obtain suitable pieces for the pot. All this of course was for commercial work.

Later on during World War One, it was a different matter. Specification alloys had to be produced. The castings made would be examined and subject to test by the Admiralty Inspectors. The castings in question were the covers which closed the opening in a mine and to which the fuses were attached. To satisfy Admiralty requirements he had to guarantee to cast six a day, each weighing about 50 lb each. This was quite an achievement in such a small building. A test bar was required with each pour and if the test bar failed then the castings would be rejected.

It soon became apparent to my father that the small building he was occupying at the rear of The White House was too small and an extension was urgently needed. A builder was engaged and plans were made for a brick building approximately 45 ft × 30 ft, with a row of windows on the south side, joined to the existing foundry. The bricklayer that the builder engaged, due to the extreme urgency, actually laid 1000 bricks a day! I believe the normal quantity of bricks to be laid by a bricklayer is between 400 and 450 today. The new building was soon complete and was a great asset. The builder, whose name was Mr Marston, was a frequent visitor to The White House for many years afterwards and became known to us all as Old Marsy.

Due to the extension of the foundry, additional labour was required. A Mr Tom Buswell, a skilled moulder who had worked with my father at S. Russell and Sons was approached; he decided that if accommodation could be found for him and his family he would join my father. It is said that when Russells knew my father was after their man, a skilled moulder, my father was chased by Dizzy Russell with a walking stick.

It so happened that an old gentleman named Sam Pallett had died and his cottage was available. Sam's cottage, now known as Horseshoe Cottage, in Snows Lane, had a thatched hovel adjoining it. As children we were warned not to go near Sam Pallett's hovel, which covered a saw pit where Sam used to work as a young man. The attraction to us was the birds' nests in the worn thatch of the roof.

Near the saw pit was a huge ancient walnut tree. The walnuts were of exceptional size and quality; the inner shells could be easily removed with bare hands. The villagers used to help themselves to the nuts and it was regarded as the village tree, but it was part of the Top Hall property where the Baxter family lived. When removing the outer skins of the walnuts we had to be careful of the stain. If Miss Sharp, our teacher, noticed this on our hands it was certain we had the cane.

   Sam's cottage was duly rented and Mr Buswell and family moved in in
1918. He had two daughters, Florrie, the eldest, and Gertrude, who
finished her schooling at the village school. Tom soon settled down in the
foundry and joined in the village life. He sang in the Church choir. He had
a beautiful tenor voice. My father's was a powerful baritone. They often
used to sing together the old songs of the day while working in the
foundry.

Keyham Village School *c.* 1925, now converted into a private house, the home of the author
and his wife.

Chapter Two

The First World War and after

During 1914 my father suddenly received his call-up papers to join the Army and was told to report for active service at the recruiting office in Leicester. This came as a great shock to my mother; by this time she had three children to support. There was much anguish and shedding of tears, but finally my father made his way on foot to Ingarsby Station to catch a train to Leicester in order to register. Just at the same time, an admiralty overseer called at the foundry. My mother explained; the overseer immediately drove off to the station where my father was still waiting for a train. My father was brought back to the foundry and instructed to continue his work, as the castings being produced were of national importance.

The fettling or finishing of the castings was undertaken by my father. This is probably the most disliked job in the foundry, especially as the only tools available in those days were a hammer, chisel, hacksaw, file and wire brushes. For some years after World War One, fettling had to be done every day after my father had delivered the previous day's work to his customers in Leicester. This often meant working until late at night. The continued handling of castings fresh out of the moulds caused my father's hands to become tough and leathery. It was a very rough job and even today with all the modern aids and machinery, fettling is an unpopular job for which it is difficult to get recruits.

The extension to the foundry made it necessary for another larger capacity furnace to be installed. A deep pit was dug and a square steel box bricked in the pit with a suitable bracket to secure the fire bars. The latter consisted of old worn files from the fettling shop, 18 ins long and known as 'three square'. The box was lined with fire bricks and connected to the chimney stack in line with the other furnaces. Unfortunately the deeper pit encountered the water-table, so that water would seep through; on one occasion it even put out the furnace fire. This problem was eventually overcome by the laying of three inch pipes from the bottom of the pit down the garden and into a ditch.

The crucibles from all the furnaces had to be lifted out by hand, as there were no lifting facilities until later.

One day when I was about four years old, I wanted to get into the

13

foundry but I was not tall enough to reach the latch. I called out, 'Bill, open the door and let me in'. No response. I banged on the door again shouting 'Bill, open the door and let me in'. Bill at last came to the door and said, 'If you want to come in you must ask me properly saying, "Please Mr Lester will you open the door?"' Feeling a bit sheepish I complied. The door was opened and I was admitted. Mr Lester worked for my father for more than twenty-five years. When I started work I was often in daily contact with him but I never after that called him by his Christian name, although everyone else did. It was a lesson in manners I never forgot.

It was soon necessary for my father to have transport of his own for delivering castings into town and so a horse and trap was acquired. The horse's name was Sparky and he occupied the stable and coach house adjacent to the front of The White House. Sparky was a quiet hard working pony and was great favourite with us children; we used to have rides on him in the paddock. Occasionally at weekends my mother and father and family would take a trip into the countryside for a picnic.

My parents were early risers and my father would work for two or three hours in the foundry and then come in for breakfast, bringing with him a list of castings which were to be delivered that day. My mother would enter the items in the despatch book in triplicate, stating the part number, customer, quantity, grade of metal and the weight of the castings. Castings

Robert, Rowles, Cissie, Mavis and Ethelwyne in a pump liner casting in 1921. A gun metal liner weighing 1,000 lbs, and the largest casting carried out by the foundry.

were sold by weight in those days at so much per pound. My father would come in and have his breakfast, wash and change, and put on his shirt with starched fronts and stiff collar, and suit complete with bowler hat. Off he would go into Leicester with Sparky leading the way. He looked very smart. On his return late in the afternoon he would change into his working clothes and go back into the foundry often until 7 or 8 o'clock at night.

Having a foundry almost on the rear doorstep is far from ideal. Foundry work is a dirty trade. The black sand used for moulding was traipsed into the kitchen on our boots especially in winter time, even though we had scrapers outside the door. My mother had her work cut out keeping the house clean and looking after her young family. One of the problems was the shortage of hot water. We had a big kitchen range with a steel fender in front. This was kept shiny and bright with emery paper and was one of my jobs. At weekends we shut down the kitchen range for baths. This was quite a business. All the flues had to be raked out and the soot removed, and the flue lids brushed out with special brushes. The fire was stoked up and shut at the top. It would roar like an express train when everything was in place and we soon had plenty of hot water for baths for the whole family.

One day my father came home with a huge copper kettle, which held at least one and a half gallons of water. It had been specially made for him by a copper-smith in Bond Street, Leicester, who was one of his customers. From then on, the kettle was always kept full on the hob, and when put on the fire it soon boiled. This was a great asset and much admired by visitors, and solved the hot water problem.

Lighting the foundry with oil lamps was far from satisfactory. My father decided to do something about this and acquired a second hand oil engine, a three and a half horse power Campbell. This would drive a small dynamo which would provide about fifteen 60 watt lamps at 110 volts DC. Three of these would be wired to the house, one in the kitchen, one in each front room, and the rest in the foundry. A Mr Bramley of Houghton on the Hill, a skilled electrician, did the wiring and fixed the dynamo. A wooden shed was built adjoining the foundry to accommodate the engine. This installation proved quite successful but as there were no storage batteries we had to use the oil lamps in the house when the engine stopped and the foundry closed down for the night. The ignition on the engine was provided in those days by an oil lamp arrangement, part of the engine. This had to be lit about 15 minutes before the engine was started and this heated a probe. One night when my father was some distance away one of the men called him urgently as something seemed to be wrong. The engine was running too fast, the lights were getting brighter and brighter. When he arrived and opened the engine house door the engine was racing even faster, and vibrating so that any minute it would tear itself from the foundations. My father hesitated for a moment as it seemed too dangerous to go near it. Finally he crawled on his hands and knees, reached out and

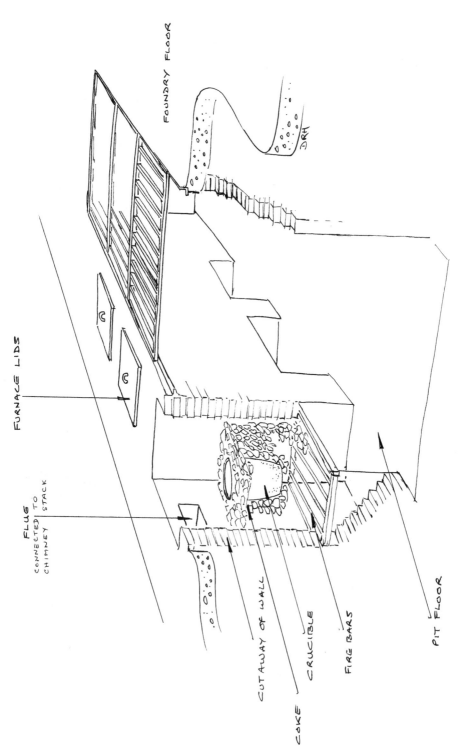

FURNACE LIDS

FOUNDRY FLOOR

FLUG
CONNECTED TO
CHIMNEY STACK

CUT AWAY OF WALL

COKE

CRUCIBLE

FIRE BARS

PIT FLOOR

Three natural draught coke-fired pit furnaces, as installed in the 'Foundry in the Garden', with cutaway section showing crucible in position. Crucibles were used to prevent products of combustion coming into contact with non-ferrous metals (see page 8).

The company's first employees at Keyham, *c.* 1923. Standing, L to R: Tom Smith, Clarrie Timson, Tom Buswell. Seated: Bert Sanderson, Len Perkins, Les Newcombe.

The author's father and mother with his two sisters Cissie and Mavis and brother Robert ready for 'the off' in the pony and trap with 'Sparky' between the shafts, 1915.

turned off the ignition lamp. Apparently the belt driving the ball-type governors had broken. The engine was out of control and would have wrecked itself if it hadn't been stopped. Fortunately no serious damage was done apart from a bent connecting rod.

During the middle of the First World War a very important casting was ordered by Messrs Gimson and Company; this was a very hush hush job only to be referred to as 'PV'. The castings had to be made in a metal called Manganese Bronze, a difficult metal to cast in those days. The first casting made proved to be faulty and had to be scrapped. The second casting was successful and was needed so urgently, it was collected from the foundry before it had cooled down. We learnt afterwards that the PV was part of a powerful shear for cutting mine cables; when severed, the mines floated to the surface where they could be disposed of. This mechanism was known as a Paravane hence PV. Improved versions are I believe still in use today.

During this period when the foundry was working late one night, the Zeppelins came over. My father was called to put out the lights and I was told that their engines could be plainly heard as they passed over to bomb Loughborough. The explosion of the bombs could also be heard. On the way back I believe one was shot down at Potters Barr.

After the war cast bronze memorial tablets were in demand to commemorate the fallen. My father was commissioned to cast one to commemorate an Australian soldier killed in battle. This depicted the figure of the soldier raised in relief and the figure of an ostrich on one side and a kangaroo on the other. The pattern or model which was provided for us to work from was made of plaster of paris and plasticine. It was a work of art. This pattern was moulded by Tom Buswell. It had to be false-cored – a term well known to foundrymen of that era. When completed Tom was much congratulated on the finish and detail. It was mounted in Peterborough Cathedral and can still be seen inside on the right of the main entrance. Many others were cast over the years, one as a memorial to the fallen of the tramways department. This used to be mounted at the entrance of the old tram depot in Humberstone Gate. Another was in memory of boys who had been students of the City Boys School and had lost their lives in the Great War. This was mounted to form an archway over the entrance to the school.

The output of the castings from the foundry was increasing and was getting a bit too much for Sparky the pony. My father reluctantly had to part with him and we were all very sad to see him go, as he had become one of the family. In his place a new half-ton Ford Van was acquired. This was a Model T Ford, and purchased from Cartwrights in Applegate Street, a Ford agent. When my father went to collect it Mr Cartwright said, 'I will drive you over the Clock Tower and then you should be all right'. This was all the instruction he had. My father arrived home safe and I can recall him saying that he knew one way to stop it and that was to switch off the ignition.

Many of the bronze tablets were ordered by the Dryad metal works who

Clarrie Timson at work in the foundry at Keyham, *c.* 1930.

were the main contractors. The metal department was in the charge of Mr George Pick who lived at Scraptoft. Sometimes on a Saturday he would be driving home in his horse and trap fast asleep in the middle of the road along Scraptoft Lane. My father would come up behind him in his van and give a toot on the horn before he could get by. George would wake up with a start and pull onto one side.

Gimsons Engineers of Vulcan Road, Leicester became our main customer whom we relied on for our bread and butter. Mr Jeffson the Managing Director of the firm seemed to take a liking to my father and after a time called him by his Christian name 'Bob'. He was disliked by the rank and file at Gimsons, because of his bullying ways. He was known as old Jeff. I think he appreciated the way my father was always willing to oblige Gimsons often working late, and through weekends and holidays. Gimsons specialised in repair work and breakdowns. This had to be undertaken other than in their customers' working hours. Jeffson told my father to go and introduce himself to an engineering firm at Newark, Messrs Worthington Simpsons, makers of pumps etc. They were very busy, although they had their own brass foundry. Jeffson may have put in a word for my father because after a couple of visits my father was rewarded with a big order. This was for several tons of castings, delivery over six months.

This extra business entailed the construction of two new furnaces which had a capacity of 300 lbs each. These were necessary because of the extra weight of some of the castings. In order to avoid previous problems with the water entering the pits these two extra furnace pits were about four feet underground and extended 18 inches above ground. This meant that after the crucible of molten metal was lifted out of the furnace and stood into its casting vuel, it had to be lowered 18 ins to the foundry sand floor.

Two men would lift the single end while my father lifted the double end. It was a perilous business. As a schoolboy I used to watch from a safe distance, trembling with fear until the metal was safely poured into the moulds. Soon after, a 5 cwt swivel crane was installed with a hand operated winch. This enabled the crucible to be safely lifted out and on to the floor.

A panoramic view of Keyham in 1908.

Chapter Three

Village and Family Life

My mother and father had little reason to chastise us children when we were young. We were generally well behaved, but sometimes my brother and I would quarrel. If this ended in a fight followed by a crying bout my father would march us off and put us in the outside toilet. He would hold the latch so that we could not get out. It was pitch dark inside with no windows, just a very small ventilator at the top. There we would stay until we quietened down. We were made to promise to behave before he would open the door and let us out. This proved to be a very effective punishment.

Our outside toilet was an old fashioned affair, a pan closet. Normally the pan is let in the floor a few inches but ours was on ground level. This meant the seat had to be built up higher. It was a real high stepper, a wide side by side two seater, and as children we had to jump to get on. You could imagine you were riding side saddle with your legs swinging in the air. One night when I had paid a visit a big rat jumped out from the seat and bolted out of the door. After that we always kicked the wooden front to make sure we were alone.

My mother was sometimes hard pressed to provide for us all and one day a nearby farmer, who went to market on Wednesdays asked my father if he would like him to buy him a pig. My father thought this was a good idea especially as there was a pig sty at the bottom of the garden. My mother had seen how the salting and curing was carried out whilst living with her parents at Woodford Halse. They always killed a pig each year for their own use. My mother was confident she could handle the curing side all right. The pig duly arrived. When the bill was presented my mother noticed that the amount had been altered from £1 to £1.10s. My father was furious. He was not easily put out but this was a case of being deliberately deceived by a farmer for whom he had often done a good turn. My father swore at him. His wife hearing the rumpus and bad language came out and said 'What is he doing to you Mr Harrison?' A few days later the farmer came round very subdued. He had apparently been to his solicitor to see if he could summons my father for using bad language, but the solicitor had advised him to apologise to my father. The ten shillings was duly paid over.

21

The pig grew rapidly. It had hot bran and potato mash every day and other leavings from the household greens. I got very attached to Snorty and it was my job to clean him out. Winter was approaching and the time was coming when the pig had to meet its end. Snorty weighed about 14 stone, just about the right weight to provide two nice sides of bacon and two hams. Sticking a pig was an unpleasant business. Preparations were made in the early morning. The copper in the wash-house was filled with water and the fire lit to provide plenty of boiling water to scald the pig.

The butcher, Mr North, arrived from the nearby village of Beeby, bringing his tools. He looked around and asked for 'the scratch'. My father did not know what he meant by this. He was soon enlightened. Luckily we had a carpenter working on the premises, and plenty of timber, and under the butcher's instructions a 'scratch' was constructed. This consisted of a strong stretcher-like object on four legs with two handles at each end. The butcher was delighted, remarked it was the best he had ever used. Off we went to the pig sty, my father, Bill from the foundry and the butcher. I was watching from a safe distance. It is said that a pig can smell a butcher and I can quite believe this. The pig squealed murder as soon as the butcher looked over the sty. The butcher quickly tied a rope in his mouth over its nose and it was quite a struggle for three men to get the pig up the garden and onto the scratch, its place of execution. Finally, with the three men holding it down, the butcher got out his knife and cut its throat. The blood curdling squeals were heard all over the village, gradually dying down as it breathed its last. I think we were all upset about this, apart from the butcher. Bill said he would never take part in anything like this again, although there was nothing unusual in this method of killing a pig in villages.

After the scalding of the pig it was taken out of the wooden trough and hung up outside on a hook upside down. Its head and offal was removed, and the rest was left until later in the evening when the butcher would come round to cut it up to our requirements. On his arrival it was taken inside and placed on a large table and out would come his knives and then it was taken into the dairy ready for the curing process. The pig's head was hung in the doorway of the wash-house outside. Later when my father and mother were going to bed they heard a bump and went outside and found that the pig's head was missing. They searched around; my father eventually went out into the street and there was the pig's head on the doorstep of the farm next door. Apparently their collie dog had managed to get if off the hook and carried it home. Fortunately it was unmarked and undamaged. The collie stood there watching whilst it was taken back.

In a small village when a family killed a pig, it was the usual practice to share in the offal. My mother was familiar with the custom. She would prepare on a large dinner plate various items of fry. This would be covered with a clean white cloth and I used to take it around the village to the lucky recipients. Rearing and killing and curing your own pig was quite an achievement.

During rationing in the war having a large orchard was a godsend. My father would see that in the autumn the apples were carefully gathered and stored in the loft and some of these were such good keepers they would keep until apples were on the tree next year. My mother used to say she did not know how she could have managed without this fruit. One year my father sent a large barrel of apples to the soldiers in the trenches for which he received a grateful letter.

As children our main meal for breakfast was what we called Quacks. I have never been able to find out how it got its name. To make it, you take a basin and break up a slice or more of bread, pour on boiling water, cover with a saucer and allow to soak, then drain off the water, add a lump of butter, and mix thoroughly adding salt and pepper. This provided us with a nourishing meal and we seemed to thrive on it. I found out afterwards it was known as 'tea kettle broth'.

My mother was an excellent needlewoman and made many of my sisters' clothes. In addition she used to visit a second-hand shop in Leicester, kept by a Mrs Roberts who had an excellent connection with the residents of Stoneygate. Many well-off people lived in that area in those days and would pass on the childrens' clothes as they grew out of them. I spent many hours with my mother in the shop while she bargained and sorted things out. The shop was dimly lit with one gas light. Even some of the second-hand clothes were too expensive for my mother to buy. I remember coming home one day with a beautiful navy blue suit with hardly a mark on it. It lasted me for years wearing it only on Sundays. We were told by my mother that if anyone asked us where our clothes came from we were to say 'Crows' (a well-known childrens' outfitter near Bond Street, Leicester). Mrs Roberts had two sons, who kept a high class gents outfitters in Halford Street.

To help my mother with the family chores, my father one day came home with a brand-new washing machine. As you can imagine it was very different from today's machines. It must have been one of the very first. It was hand operated, a big cumbersome thing on wheels. It had the usual mangle mounted on the top with six inch diameter rollers operated by a hand wheel. Inside the wooden body was a rotating metal cage with a lift off lid. This cage held the clothes. The boiling water had to be carried from the copper in the wash-house. It took 8 gallons. The clothes were put in the cage and the lid closed, and washing commenced. A geared arrangement connected to the handle to rotate the cage. It was hard work turning the handle about 50 to 60 revolutions a minute. Leslie from the foundry was allowed to help on washdays and of course my brother and I would be made to take our turn. The machine was effective if the handle was turned for a reasonable time. The handle could be reversed, so it was easy to unwind the clothes which became tangled up. The water was drained out from a tap at the bottom through a hosepipe into a drain. For the rinse the machine had to be re-filled with cold water from the tap at the sink. (This supply came from the soft water tank in the bathroom.) The machine was well made and lasted for a number of years; it was a great improvement on the old rubbing board and dolly pegs but still laborious.

When my father acquired the Ford van, news soon got around the village. After he became proficient in driving, my mother would go into town and some of the family too. This was a great improvement on the pony and trap, especially in bad weather. There were no windscreen wipers in those days, the window had to be tilted or swivelled upwards to enable the driver to see underneath it when it rained. Afterwards a hand operated wiper became available.

It was soon apparent that there would be requests for rides into town and my father, always willing and ready to oblige, fixed some seats in the back of the van and charged 6d each way for anyone wanting a ride when he happened to be going in for his deliveries. The only other means of transport was to beg a ride in a farmer's pony and trap, or walk to Ingarsby, one and a half miles away, and go by train. After a time some of his passengers got to know where his customers were situated and would wait outside for a ride on his return journey. He had to put a stop to this and told them that they would only be picked up at a certain stopping place. My father was always known to his customers by his Christian name Robert or Bob. My mother always called him Bert and other relations also.

The clerical side of the foundry business was all undertaken by my mother, book keeping, invoicing, correspondence and so on. It was amazing how she managed to get through the work. I can remember her once saying 'I wonder what Gimsons would say if they could see me making out their account and nursing a baby'. The end of each month was the busiest time when all the accounts had to be out.

Having acquired a motor van, supplies of petrol were required. This was available in towns from hand operated pumps. However, a local supply became available. Petrol and paraffin were delivered by a wagon drawn by two horses. The wagon carried a large tank of paraffin: on two brass taps at the rear hung the two five-gallon measures. The two-gallon cans of petrol would be carried on racks on each side of the wagon. My father would require perhaps 50 gallons of paraffin which was tipped into a large storage tank in the shed in the yard. This was needed for the oil lamps in the foundry and the house. The paraffin was sold to anyone in the village. He would buy 12 two-gallon tins of petrol, called Pratts, priced 1/6d per gallon with 3/- on the can. As more cars came on the roads it was not unusual to have callers from time to time who would run out of petrol. 'Could you please let me have some petrol, I've run short on Keyham hill.' A can would be produced. 'That will be 3/- and 3/- on the can.' 'Oh er I am sorry I have only got 1/10d on me.' 'In that case I will see if I have an empty can and let you have half'. 'Thank you very much, you are kind. Could you lend me a funnel please,' 'Yes, but you must bring it straight back, and the petrol can, there is 3/- on the can.' That's the last we would see of him. Over the years this happened many times, so usually I would be told to tag along to bring the can back.

My father often used to lend his chimney-sweeping brushes to neighbours but in spite of instructions they would get the brush detached and stuck in the chimney. This usually meant that a builder would have to climb on the roof and dangle a weight on a rope down the chimney to dislodge it.

Sometimes the neighbours must have found the adjacent foundry a trial. Near neighbours sometimes had to take in their washing because of smuts – usually on Monday morning. To get over this we stopped casting yellow brass on Mondays. When this metal overheated it would give off a dense white snow-like fume. This soon cleared after pouring ceased. But there were few complaints about fumes and noise, perhaps because my father was very popular in the village and willing to help others especially with transport.

Mr & Mrs Archer who occupied the thatched cottage near the church had two sons, Eric and Jimmy. Jimmy was the daring one of the family, always up to something and taking all manner of risks. Jimmy was often watching through the foundry windows and one day he asked me to let him have some moulding sand. He wanted to make something in his shed at the rear of his house. After making the mould he melted some scrap lead in a cocoa tin on the kitchen fire and after casting his mould, poured the remainder of the lead onto the concrete floor outside. It had been

Keyham, main street looking towards the school, *c.* 1908.

raining and there was a terrific explosion, poor Jimmy was splashed in the face by the molten lead. Luckily his eyes escaped but his face bore witness of the mishap for several weeks. On another occasion while watching a farmer breaking slabs of cow-cake in the hand operated machine, Jimmy got his fingers in the cogs of the machine and was taken to the Infirmary for treatment. After his hand got better, when the head mistress Miss Sharpe gave him the cane this was always on his bad hand.

There were five small farms in the village: mostly dairy farms. Commencing at the lower part of the village, Pear Tree Farm was rented by Mr and Mrs Sam Greaves, an elderly couple, with their two sons, Tom and Frank, and two daughters. Tom joined the forces during World War One and came back safe. Frank did not go to the war because he was a cripple, but was able to help his father on the farm. I can remember Mr Sam Greaves coming down the steps of his farm with his gun. He had a very large beard and he would walk down the lane and into one of his fields known as The Dairy Grounds where there was a large rabbit warren. This warren was covered with nettles and he would sit down about ten yards away with his gun at the ready and wait for a rabbit to come out. He didn't have long to wait and was soon back with one for the pot. He did not like anyone to trespass in his fields. He would shout and rave and if they did not move out he would unchain his dog Bogy to send after them. Sam's unmarried daughters, Daisy and Nellie, would occupy the school after school on Fridays and sell war savings certificates to help the war effort.

Keyham, main street from the churchyard, c. 1942. *(a post-war car in the street!)*

West End Farm was rented by Mr and Mrs Jack Sanderson. They came to live in the village soon after my father. This was the farm where we were able to obtain our milk. I would sometimes have to wait while he finished milking the cows and the milk would then be put through a linen cloth into a churn. After a stir in the churn it would be measured into my can, the milk still warm. After a cow had calved we would be favoured with the first milk. This was called beestings. My mother made this into a traditional pudding similar to an egg custard.

The house now known as Blackthorn Farm was occupied by the Burton family. Mr Burton ran a small-holding when he wasn't in the Dog and Gun. There were eight children, four boys and four girls. Jack, the eldest, joined the Royal Flying Corps during the war. Dorothy the eldest girl stayed at home helping with the housework. I was at school with Tom and have kept in touch with him from time to time. He is now 89. The Burton family had a trap with a horse called Taffy. Tom told me his father was well known in the locals in the nearby villages. He used to travel around in the horse and trap and Taffy always managed to get him home safe although he was often asleep. One day he was asked to loan Taffy to a certain titled lady for a day's hunting. This did not work out at all well because Taffy instead of following the hounds, stopped at every pub he came to. Taffy, was a great favourite with the family and was used regularly by Mrs Burton to take her into Leicester.

Keyham, cottages at junction of Kings Lane and Main Street, showing gate leading to 'The Fold', 1908. Kings Lane was orignally known as Cowslip Lane.

One Christmas when there was a blizzard that lasted for days, it was so bad no tradesmen were able to call. The roads were blocked by huge snow drifts and Tom told me he and his mother had nothing to eat for Christmas Day (by then, his father had died and his sisters were away working in domestic service). Tom, aged twelve, decided to walk to Leicester over the fields and snowdrifts to visit an Aunt. He walked back having been provided with a chicken or something. He was completely exhausted.

Garfoots were the bakers at Houghton on the Hill, they normally delivered to Keyham every other day, by horse and cart, but during the bad blizzard of March 1917 the roads were blocked and the only access to the village was across the fields. Mr Garfoot came on horse-back carrying the bread in a sack on his back.

Mayfield Farm opposite the Church was a dairy farm and run by the Timson family. Mr Timson was a retired builder (who helped build my father's foundry); the farm was run by his son Sidney. They kept about ten cows. The family consisted of five sons and three daughters. Tom and Jack were soldiers during the War. Clarence, always known as Clarrie, had a crippled foot due to a fall at an early age, and walked with a crutch. He was a remarkable man, always cheerful and never letting his disability affect him. As a boy he loved to climb trees, buildings and even the church tower. My father employed him from the age of fourteen in the foundry at Keyham. He

The Timson family who occupied Mayfield Farm, c. 1915.
Left to right, back row: Emily, Sidney, Tom, Doris. Middle row: Father with Connie, Mother with Roy. Front row: Ethel, Clarrie, who worked for the Harrison family for over 50 years.

was trained as a coremaker, a job which enabled him to sit at a bench. Clarrie was first up on the foundry roof to get a good view when the hounds were about. His crutch was made out of an old hay fork but with a straight piece of wood at the top. On the bottom was a brass ferrule. This crutch served him for much of his life. Clarrie worked for my father at Keyham and then in Leicester at Gough Road for more than 50 years. He was trained as a moulder after his work in the village, and became very skilled. His work was of particular importance during World War Two when the castings he was making were for the Ministry of Air Craft production. I cannot praise too highly his skill, ability, and willingness. Clarrie outlived his brothers and sisters and died in 1990 at the age of 88. His brother Roy, the youngest of the family, also became a foundryman, at Keyham and Leicester. The daughters, Ethel, Doris and Connie were all in domestic service.

In May 1913 I had reached the age of five and it was time for me to start school. The village school was only 100 yds away and I was waiting with my mother to hear the first sounds of the school bell. This was usually rung by the teacher at 10 minutes to nine. I did not like the idea at all of school; who would, when all the wonderful scenes at the rear of the house were taking place. Queer shapes made of sand and metal, molten metal being lifted out of a hole in the ground in pots and poured into a mould. I used to stand and stare through the windows. It was all so interesting and fascinating, but school it had to be. I was very nervous, my mother took my hand and off we went at the sound of the bell. I was introduced to the teacher, a Miss Sharp. Living near the school I was able to come home for lunch and join the rest of the family.

The school hours were 9am to 12noon one and a half hours for lunch and finishing at 3.45pm. I did not settle very well, and was always glad when it was time to go home.

The school lavatory and washing facilities were primitive in the extreme. There was no running water. The pump at the rear of the school was rarely used, although there was a small wash basin behind the door in the porch. I cannot remember any towels being available.

The school playgrounds were divided into two by a five foot wall, the girls on one side which had a grass surface and boys on the other which had a gravel surface. The usual ball games were played. The balls often went over the hedge into Miss Healey's garden, which caused her great annoyance. When the balls were returned they were often punctured or sometimes she would keep them until we summoned up enough courage to call in the shop to collect them.

Our school teacher, Miss Edith Sharpe, had been appointed head mistress of Keyham school on January 13th 1908. She was a strict disciplinarian and most of her scholars made good progress with their education. She would line us up each morning at 9am when the weather was fine, in two lines outside the school porch, boys on one side and girls on the other. At a given signal we would march in and settle in our places. While she marked the register our names would be called out one by one

The author and his brother Robert, photograph taken towards the end of the First World War, outside the village school, Keyham.

and we would reply 'present'. This would be followed by a hymn and a short reading from the Bible. Miss Sharpe had an unenviable task; the teaching of 30–40 pupils aged between five and fourteen. Later she had the assistance of a pupil teacher, a girl in the sixth form at the school, Miss Ida Fairbrother who lived at Beeby. Miss Fairbrother was given a half day off each week to further her studies. In the school playground was a flag pole and on Empire day, May 24th, we would be assembled outside in the playground and be given a talk about the empire. We sang patriotic songs and the flag was hoisted. We would march past saluting it. Miss Sharpe was very patriotic and would get angry and upset when bad news was reported in the press regarding the progress of the war. On such occasions we knew what was likely to follow; someone would get a caning. The teacher always kept the cane exhibited and was not slow in bringing it to use, normally two or three strokes on the hand. One little girl of only seven received two strokes for telling a lie. Children as young as five received the cane.

Miss Sharpe was courting Billy Ward whose father Leonard kept the Dog and Gun. Billy had enlisted as a soldier, leaving his aged father on his own, his mother having died earlier. Sometimes if Miss Sharpe saw Mr Ward taking a walk up Snows Lane she would send one of us out of the school with a chair for him to have a rest. A year or two later the old man died and the tenancy of the Dog and Gun became available. It was always understood that his son would take over the tenancy, but being away at War he could not do this. (Apart from being a licensee he had a small-holding of about 30 acres.) So instead of Billy, Mr Tunnicliffe, who was on the staff at Baggrave Hall, became the new tenant. Great resentment was felt in the village when this change came about, and Miss Sharpe was particularly bitter. I remember when we were asked to write an essay about the war, I spelt the word soldier wrong. As a result of this I was given the cane.

The school had regular visits by the school attendance officer. He would call out anyone with bad attendance figures in front of the class and give them a good talking to. He would also at times visit their homes to see their parents. I think Miss Sharpe looked forward to his visits. Sometimes he would stop for half an hour or so and they would stand together behind her desk and suddenly burst into muffled laughter. I heard one of the boys say, 'I bet that was a good one'.

In 1917, during the War, Miss Sharpe was instructed by the Ministry of Munitions to arrange for the children at Keyham School to collect as many of the horse chestnuts as possible. Keyham had a wonderful avenue of trees in the old days and the children were given time from their lessons to do this. We collected six 1-cwt sacks. They were stored in the porch of the school where they remained for several months. Finally they were collected. We were told they would be used in the manufacture of explosives. I have since discovered that conkers played a curious but significant role in World War One. A serious shortage of acetone, a solvent employed in the manufacture of the explosive Cordite, caused David Lloyd George, at the time Minister of Munitions, to seek the help of the great Zionist Chaim Weizmann of Manchester University who isolated the bacterium that would convert starch to acetone. Forced to abandon maize as a source of starch due to the reductions in imports caused by German submarines, Weizmann, who was a director of Admiralty laboratories, used conkers, apparently very abundant in the Autumn of 1917. The collection, mainly by children, was organised nationally as it was again in World War Two. The school children were also asked to collect blackberries for the army and the navy but decided to withdraw from this scheme because of the difficulty of getting them to the town.

One day during the early years of the war a small aeroplane came over the village flying very low, diving and sweeping over the houses turning his engine on and off. This went on for about 10 minutes. Clarrie Timson who was working in the foundry at the time was as usual first on the roof to get a good view. I doubt whether anyone in the village had seen an aeroplane before; I certainly hadn't. Finally the engine was shut off and it glided down to land in what we knew as the Bullock Field. The pilot made a good landing but on the forward run it tipped up on its nose. The propeller and undercarriage was badly damaged. The pilot was unhurt.

We all ran to the scene; our teacher Miss Sharpe was one of the first to reach it. The pilot was removing his flying helmet as she arrived; she excitedly cried out 'Why, its Jack Burton'. Jack had been to school at Keyham and was always her favourite pupil.

Jack had been sent out on a practice flight from his base and decided to visit his mother whose garden adjoined the Bullock Field. Jack dare not call at his home under the circumstances, so made his way to the Top Hall. The people there informed his base by telegram and put him up for the night. Jack's excuse was that he had to make a forced landing due to engine trouble. His mother had gone into Leicester at the time with Taffy and the trap. Someone must have informed her what had happened. She immediately returned home; poor Taffy was whipped as never before. He broke all records for a pony and trap travelling from Leicester to Keyham. He had never been treated like this before.

The plane was too badly damaged to take off and eventually had to be dismantled and taken away on a lorry. In the meantime part of the plane suspension, which was made of strong elastic, we boys made into catapults.

During December 1918 Miss Sharpe was taken ill. Mrs Tunnicliffe, from the Dog and Gun, was engaged as a temporary substitute. Although she had no teaching qualifications she was a good disciplinarian and kept us in order. When it was realised that Miss Sharpe's illness was very serious, and that it was unlikely that she would be able to resume her duties, a new teacher, Miss Potter, was engaged early in 1919. She was a maiden lady of about sixty years of age. She proved to be an excellent teacher; much appreciated by parents and children. Miss Potter lodged with Miss Healey. Soon after this we heard that Miss Sharpe had married Billy Ward, but were shocked to hear a few months after that she had died of throat cancer. Miss Potter stayed on as Headmistress until 1921. During that time there were occasions when she was ill with nervous problems. Miss Healey asked her to find other accommodation as the shop and post office were taking up most of her time. My mother was concerned as there was talk of Miss Potter's resignation. She got up a successful petition to try to persuade her to stay, obtaining the signatures of other mothers in the village and outlying farms. My mother provided her with accommodation, she stayed with us at The White House until 1921 when she resigned owing to ill health. Mrs Tunnicliffe again took over until the new teacher was engaged. Mrs Tunnicliffe had a daughter, Miriam, she was an only child and was brought up to think herself better than the rest of us. She went to Keyham school for a number of years and then on to the Alderman Newton Girls School. Her father Ernest, bought her a horse to enable her to follow the hounds with the Quorn. Villagers used to say 'Look there's Miriam pushing herself in front on her old nag'. It was believed that it was her mother's hope that she would meet someone in the hunting field. This never came about and she spent most of her time behind the bar in the Dog and Gun, and remained a spinster.

Keyham school *c.* 1950, used as a pattern store by R.C. Harrison & Son Ltd. To the right of the photograph is the wall that segregated the boys from the girls in the playground.

A crucible used in the Keyham Foundry, now serving as a container for growing herbs, in the authors garden.

The village school room was the centre of the social life in Keyham and was available for hire by the educational authorities for the sum of 10s for functions such as dances, whist drives, concerts, or meetings. The school desks were nine to ten feet long and had to be moved outside into the playground when dances took place. The desks had cast iron ends and cast iron centres and required two strong men to move them. The desk top was adjustable and set at an angle. Small porcelain inkwells were let into the desk tops.

Most of the desks were left in the room for whist drives and it was like an obstacle race jumping over them when the bell rang to change seats. The room itself was 24 ft square and it was provided with a large cast iron coal fired stove in an alcove at one side of the room. It had two small doors which opened at the front. The teacher on a cold day would open the doors and then sit in front on her chair. The rest of us were perished. In fact, sometimes during a very cold winter the ink in the wells would be frozen and therefore couldn't be used. We would then have to use slates and chalk.

Some of the children came from outlying farms and had to travel 1 or 2 miles. One family who lived at a farm near Beeby always went home for lunch and were always back within the one and a half hours allowed for lunch.

Keyham School was built during 1885 at a cost of £420 for the building. It was built on land once owned by the Miles family and was to accommodate 45 children and 14 infants, an average attendance of thirty.

The school closed on February 28th 1939, by which time only nine children attended. Three children went to Thurnby and six to Hungarton. The school re-opened during the war to cater for the education of evacuees from London who were billeted with various families in the village.

Many horses were in use on the farms in Keyham before and during the First World War. This necessitated the regular visit of a stud stallion; these came sometimes from Tilton on the Hill, sometimes elsewhere. The attendants who walked with them would be smartly dressed in corduroy breeches, highly polished leggings and boots and tweed cap. The stallions were decorated with ribbons and prize winning medals, beautifully groomed with tails plaited – a wonderful sight as they paraded down the village street. We boys would shout 'Hi, here comes the stally man' and we would follow down Snows Lane, keeping our distance, to just below Pear Tree Farm. Here was a gate which led into the cricket field. This was the place for serving mares.

The mare was in the field with the farmer and the gate closed. After mare and stallion were introduced and became friendly, the stally man would open the gate to put them together in the field. This was where we would be told by the stally man, with a crack of his whip, to clear off.

The farm at the top of the village known as The Fold was occupied and farmed by the Johnson family: Mr Johnson, his wife Sarah, Norman his son and his daughters, Frances and Alice. Norman and I were great

The Quorn Hunt at Keyham, *c.* 1950.

Garden Fete at Nether Hall 1950. Muriel with the twins in a "twin pram".

friends and went to school together. Mr Johnson was church warden for many years at Keyham Church and when the church bells were re-cast during 1926 his name was cast in raised letters on one of the bells. Teddy specialised in sheep rearing and after the lambing season his services were in great demand locally. When the time came due for the castration of the lambs, after operating on his own lambs he would oblige other farmers. I won't go into too much detail about his method except to say that his only tools were a small sharp knife and his sharp teeth.

Our village Church, All Saints Keyham, was in the diocese of Rothley and was well attended. The vicar, Revd Pearson, used to cycle from Rothley each Sunday evening to take the services. He was a school master for many years before taking up the ministry. He made regular visits to the parishioners in the village and called in at the school to address a few words to the children. He visited my mother and was known to say that she always taught him something. My mother was well versed with the Bible. He was also known to visit the Dog and Gun after the church service and remonstrate with the occupants to try to get them to come to Church. During 1926, whilst coming to take the church service at Keyham on his cycle, he was killed.

Nether Hall was occupied by the Freer family during the early part of World War One, and their two daughters were born there. Mr Freer was a Solicitor who practised in Leicester and the domestic staff consisted of a cook, two maids, and a handyman named Turner who looked after the garden and acted occasionally as chauffeur. The Freers were then the only people in the village who owned a car.

Turner would watch the moulders at work through one of the foundry windows and he had an idea to try and make a mould and cast an ignition key in lead of his boss's car. To form the moulding box he used two inside parts of a matchbox with the bottoms removed. For sand he used very fine garden soil. The lead was melted on the kitchen fire and after several attempts, and after much filing and trimming, the key would fit the car.

On the staff's day off they would walk to Ingarsby Station and catch a train into Leicester. Turner would make arrangements to meet them off the train with his boss's car and give them a ride home. He and two young men (one was Clarrie Timson), would push the car out of the garage and down the street before starting the engine. This worked several times but one night Mrs Freer looked out of the bedroom window and saw them pushing the car back into the garage. In the morning poor Turner was given a minute's notice.

Mr and Mrs Seal were next to occupy the Nether Hall, following the Freer family who moved to the Top Hall. Mr Seal was a manufacturer of elastic web material at his own factory at Whitwick. Mrs Seal played the organ for services in the church; both Mr and Mrs Seal were generous benefactors to the village. Mr Seal paid for the three church bells to be recast and rehung. The recasting was done in 1926 by the Loughborough Bell Foundry. The new bells were rehung on a steel framework.

The Old Hall, Keyham, 1908, the home of John Cross until 1910.

Mr Harris who later lived at the Nether Hall used some of the oak from the old bell frame to provide a mantlepiece in the Oak Room over the fireplace. An inscription carved on the oak read 'upon this oak Keyham bells once bore now stands here for evermore'.

The Seals had one son, Daffen, who was born in Keyham. Daffen was their pride and joy. He had a full time nanny, a qualified nurse who lived in. Daffen was taken out by the nurse in a beautiful high coach built pram, and she wore full nurse's uniform. Villagers used to say she thought more of him than the parents did. Mr Seal owned a beautiful big new saloon Sunbeam car. He was a small man and I can remember the difficulty he sometimes had turning it in and out of the hall gates; there was no power steering then.

The Seal family moved from Keyham when Daffen was three years old. I think the two Halls in Keyham were let on Lease, as I cannot remember them being unoccupied for very long.

The Baxter family were living at the Top Hall during 1914. They were merchants. Ethel, the daughter, married Henry Beecham, son of Sir Thomas Beecham, manufacturing chemist.

There was a large and very ornamental greenhouse on the right hand side of the Hall when facing it from the front. This housed a grape vine – a black hamburg. This greenhouse was heated by a solid fuel boiler which occupied the lower part of the brick building facing Kings Lane. This lane was known as Cowslip Lane in those days. The upper part of the building was used as a potting shed. The greenhouse had deteriorated badly and after the First World War it became unsafe and was pulled down. This was during Squire Hincks' time. After this the boiler house was used to store his empty wine bottles. The village boys and girls would play hide and seek in the building and would gain admittance through a small hand gate which lead to the rear of the Hall.

Originally in Keyham there were five charity cottages. One of these was sold to the proprietors of The Dog and Gun and pulled down, the proceeds being used to provide additional facilities for the remaining four cottages.

These were generally occupied by elderly people – old-age pensioners. The Kirby family lived in the one next to the Church: Mrs Kirby and her three daughters, Kathleen, Patty and Ada and one son, Robert, who was known in the village as Bob. Robert joined up in the First War and was severely wounded in the face while fighting in the trenches. Two of the girls, Kathleen and Patty, were working away from home in domestic service. Ada married Mr Horace Walker, occupying one of the charity cottages in the row near her mother. They brought up three sons, Geoffrey, Roger and Philip. Their father, an agricultural worker, was for many years a dairyman for a farmer on the Uppingham Road. At 5.30 in the morning he would be off on his Connaught motor cycle. It was said by people that they used to set their clocks by his punctuality.

After World War One Bob came back to live at Keyham. He was a good village man and acted as church warden and rang the bells for many years. He was always ready to help in village affairs, organising dances, whist drives etc. He was a member of the cricket club. He married one of the staff at the Top Hall and went to live at Barkby. He often came to Keyham to see his mother, bringing with him his wife and son George on his twin AJS motor cycle and twin sidecar. George became a foundryman and worked for my father for more than thirty years.

Patty gave up her job in service and came home to look after her mother. She was a regular church attender and after her mother died she took over the cottage where she lived for the rest of her life. She died in 1990 at the age of 92.

Chapter Four

Between the two World Wars

At the end of World War One, the inhabitants of Keyham Estate were shocked to receive notice of the changes that were to take place. The Keyham Village estate had been owned by the Miles family for about 150 years. Mr W.J. Miles, aged 45, was made bankrupt in 1903 and the estate had to be sold. His two sons Roger and Ralph were killed during the 1914–1918 war leaving one daughter named Irene who became Mrs A. Cheales. She was the last of the Miles family, and was living in South Africa. In September 1905 the estate was sold to Mr Henry Thorpe Hincks, an Auctioneer and Land Agent, who lived at Wigston Hall.

He decided to come and live at the Top Hall, Keyham, as his intention was to farm the whole estate of five farms and nine farm cottages. Also included in the estate was The Dog and Gun and the Post Office, the Blacksmiths Shop and the Slaughter House which was let to Mr Fielding of Houghton on the Hill. This sudden change was devastating to the five farmers and their farm labourers, most of whom had settled in the village for many years. Notices had been served on all the farms and those unable to find other accommodation had to arrange a sale.

The Wright family, the largest tenants, who farmed the White House Farm, were the first to go. They purchased a farm which was for sale at Ingarsby. This is still farmed by one of the same family today.

The smallholding known as Cottage Farm, the entrance to which is opposite the village Church, was occupied by a Mr and Mrs Woodford, an elderly couple. They came to Keyham around 1912 to farm this smallholding. It was part of the Keyham estate but for some reason they were allowed to carry on renting this. Mr Woodford asked my father if he would sell him the paddock which joined his land. It was agreed to sell him half for £25. This was the half which joined the School playground: it was fenced off into two parts. In due course when Mr Hincks heard of this deal, he said 'Woodford, how are you going to get access, you have no right of way, you can only get in by Aeroplane'. As children we sometimes took a short cut through a gap in the hedge into the lane through a tumble-down fence. Mr Hincks had this gap filled in and back fenced with barbed wire. Poor Mr Woodford was in a quandary, the plot became a wilderness. Eventually he made a way in, an entrance lower down where he built a pig sty on the land. Mrs Woodford kept poultry in the paddock at the back of her house, this included guinea fowls.

Mr Teddy Johnson, who lived with his family at the small farm now known as The Fold, refused to accept notice to leave and claimed he could not be turned out. He was bitterly reluctant to move and stood out to the last. Finally he had to go.

The Freer family, at the Top Hall, hearing of the changes that were taking place in the village, decided to leave. They offered the Johnsons and their son Norman the remains of their Lease. The Johnsons then moved to a small bungalow at Beeby while a modern wooden bungalow was being built near Keyham Hill. When it was finished they moved in and started farming land which they had purchased nearby.

Mr Hincks and his two charming daughters Miss Emily and Miss Kitty moved into the Hall during 1919; as the people under notice moved out of the village, his own staff moved in. Mr Hincks employed a farm bailiff, a cowman, a shepherd, a wagoner, blacksmith and farm labourers; also a bricklayer and carpenter. The domestic staff at the Hall consisted of two maids and Jock, a young man who used to serve at table at dinner, and a handyman named Harry Wyatt who had been with the family for many years.

The cook/housekeeper at the Top Hall, a Miss Drayton, whose name was Jane, would sometimes send one of the maids to ask me to attend to the Misses Hincks' radio, when it went wrong. Jane had her own room next to the kitchen; she had a huge black bushy beard. She was on the short side and rather stout. She was a jolly generous soul but anyone meeting her for the first time got quite a surprise.

Squire Hincks was six feet or more in height, broad shouldered and very upright and was often seen walking in his fields with half a dozen dogs around him. He always carried a Spud, this is a type of long handled hoe with a small blade at the end which he used to chop up the jack thistles as he walked along. Mr Hincks joined the Quorn Hunt and from time to time invited them to meet at the Top Hall.

The 1914/1918 war was over and all over the country celebrations were held. Keyham was no exception although celebrations were belated due to the wartime rationing. Mr Hincks organised a real feast for the village. There were sports for the young and old. These were held in the paddock joining the Hall. There were races for children of all ages, a sumptuous buffet lunch followed by high tea, the presentation of prizes and finally a firework display. Mr Hincks was called upon to make a speech, he thanked everyone for their attendance and gave thanks for the cessation of hostilities.

The Quorn Hunt were regular visitors to Keyham during the hunting season. My earliest recollections would be a few years before the First World War. They would pass down Snows Lane and through the gate into the Cricket field, where the small boys would rush to open the gate for them, sometimes receiving a penny. They would then pass over the bridge over the brook this being a short cut to the fox cover off Covert Lane. Nowadays they have to make a detour following the bridle road on the way to the fox cover to avoid the corn fields.

The Prince of Wales, during the thirties, would join the hunt and on one occasion was accompanied by his two brothers, the Duke of Gloucester and the Duke of Kent. They were photographed by the Leicester Mercury just below The White House.

Some of the residents living at the Hill Crest Bungalows were the first to know if the Princes were hunting. They would gather near the Beeby turn and await the arrival of the horse boxes and the Princes in their cars. They would exchange pleasantries about the weather etc. The Princes did not join the meet until the hunt moved off.

The Misses Hincks gave a wonderful Christmas party for all the children of the village up to the age of fourteen. A large tree was beautifully decorated and two presents from the tree were given to each child. Mr Hincks acted the part of Father Christmas, wearing a huge eskimo fur coat. This was his first year at Keyham. In the following years this part was played by his handyman, Harry White. These parties carried on for many years and were very much looked forward to by the children.

Around Christmas time it was usual for Squire Hincks to invite the local farmers to a Christmas Supper up at The Hall. This was very popular. My father sometimes had an invitation. Squire Hincks was a well-known wine connoisseur and had a well stocked cellar. His services were called on at special times to advise at agricultural functions. At one of these functions a cartoonist depicted the guests at a table. In front of Mr Hincks was shown a cup and saucer. He was well-known only to drink wine!

Soon Mr Hincks' own men occupied the various houses and cottages. A dairy herd was built up over the years of between 50 and 80 cows. These occupied the cow sheds of Pear Tree Farm and Blackthorn Farm. The milking was a lengthy business. The cows would be herded into the yard until milking was complete and then let out into Snows Lane, some going up the lane and some going into the field below. It is not difficult to imagine the state of the roads especially in the winter and wet weather. Some of the cows used to lick the windows of The White House trying to get at my mother's plants. The farm labourers wore hob-nailed boots and leggings.

The eviction of cottagers affected my father as two of the cottages were occupied by his workers. Mr Len Perkins decided to leave the village and return to Leicester as no accommodation could be found. My parents decided that Mr Buswell, a key man, would have to come and live with us, with his daughter Gertrude.

My father then decided he would have to provide staff accommodation himself. The village presented no suitable site to build on. Finally he was offered a plot of land in Scraptoft parish. This amounted to 16 acres; much more than he required, so about 4 acres was retained and fenced off as a building site, the rest was rented to a local farmer. Whatever the setbacks, my father was never daunted. I think this great capacity for hard work and perseverence must have impressed itself on my brother Robert and myself.

My father heard of an army sale that was being held at Belton Park near Grantham. He went there by train. It was a huge army training ground for soldiers and officers built before and during World War One. He selected a large building used for officers as a regimental institute. A figure of £200 was agreed and paid for on the spot. Shortly after the sale he was approached by two men who were also interested in the same building. He was asked if he would sell to them. My father agreed; the price would be £400. They hesitated and went away when they found out it had been sold for £200. My father was always ready for a deal. The next problem was the dismantling of the building and the transfer to Keyham. Two young men, the Rudkin brothers, Herbert and Bert, who were recently demobbed from the army and were working for my father, were sent to help with the others on the site. I asked if I could go with them; my mother reluctantly agreed. I was eleven at the time.

We were to camp out in one of the rooms, so armed with blankets and a few cooking utensils we set off by train. My job was supposed to be to pick up nails as the building was dismantled. Other men were engaged on the site. They had become very skilled and had been working on this dismantling job for some time. It was amazing how quickly they worked. The building was beautifully built with best materials, the roof principals were of pitched pine 30 ft span. The uprights 5 x 3; the whole building was lined with asbestos including the inside ceilings. I was fascinated by the skill of the men taking the large pieces of asbestos from the high ceiling. One man would lie on his back on a narrow board suspended high up under the ceiling. After the corrugated iron sheets had been taken off, another man on the outside of the roof would tap gently with a mallet to loosen the nails, while the man on the plank supported the sheet until it was loose and then handed it down to someone on the ground. One day when I was picking up nails outside the building the men on the roof were removing a big ventilator. This was unbolted and loosened and they allowed it to slide down the roof and crash on the ground below. It came down where I had been standing; fortunately I saw it coming and made a quick dash through a doorway into a room. Bert who saw what happened told the men off in no uncertain manner. They were a slap-happy lot but certainly knew how to dismantle a building. I decided that the safest time to pick up the nails was early morning before the men started work or after they had gone home for the night.

After about three days a telegram arrived to say my father had met with an accident and had broken his wrist. This was caused by a back-fire of the starting handle on the Ford. The T model Fords were notorious for this. It was a double fracture and temporarily prevented him from driving. One of the two Rudkin brothers, Herbert, had a driving licence and was instructed to return with me. The other brother Bert stayed on until the job of dismantling was complete.

When the building was completely dismantled the whole lot was put on rail and consigned to Ingarsby Station; unfortunately while on rail it was held up for six weeks by a railway strike. Eventually it was unloaded and carted by horse and wagon to the building site at Keyham.

Meantime Marsie the builder had prepared the foundations for the four bungalows, each to have four good sized rooms. They were set in pairs. In between and over the space of two pairs of bungalows a 2000 gallon water tank was mounted which caught all the water from the roofs of the four bungalows. It was lovely soft water which was shared by all.

I don't think my father had any great difficulty in getting the plans passed by the Local Council in spite of the site having no mains water, electricity or sanitary arrangements. The wooden bungalows were built on a 9 inch brick foundation with about 2 feet of airspace beneath the floors.

Fortunately the builders were provided with good drawings and gradually the first two bungalows began to take shape. A brick-built wash house complete with copper was provided for each pair of bungalows. Included in this building was a secure storage compartment for each which held 1 ton of coal. Each had its own toilet which had to be 40 or 50 yards away to comply with the sanitary laws in those days. It is said that on one occasion during a very thick fog at night one of the tenants got lost after paying a visit and found himself on the top road. The space between the toilets and the bungalows provided a garden which harvested wonderful crops of vegetables. Steps led down to the garden under a veranda which faced south. It really was an ideal place to live: conditions and facilities were if anything better than some of the cottages in the village. Generally the bungalows were occupied by families whose husbands worked in the foundry and for which they were built. There were however times when if one became available it would be let to outsiders.

I remember an occasion when one was advertised and a lady arrived from Leicester pushing a large old coach-built pram containing bonny bouncing twin boys. The poor woman was exhausted when she arrived at The White House. It was my job to show her round the bungalow. She was so tired she asked me if I would push the pram up Snows Lane, which I did, feeling very embarrassed and hoping no one would see me. The rent was 12 shillings a week which included rates.

My father's wrist was mending and though still in a sling, he was driving again. The foot controls on the Model T Fords made this possible. One snag was he could not sound the hooter. This suited me for I was delegated to sit on the front seat with the hooter on my knee. This meant a holiday from school. The hooter was a bulbous rubber type. My father had to calm me down when I became too enthusiastic.

It soon became apparent that a drinking water supply would have to be provided for the bungalows and the only way to do this would be to sink a well. The local grave digger, named Archie and 70 years of age, was engaged. A young man named Leslie who worked in the foundry and myself were delegated to help. A suitable site was chosen; a hand operated winch was acquired and positioned over the spot. Leslie and I were above ground operating the winch hauling up the spoil, while Archie was doing the digging. A hole about 4 feet in diameter took shape. It was surprising how quickly we progressed until after about 10 feet blue clay was encountered and this slowed up the digging somewhat. After about ten days we had a hole thirty foot deep but as no sign of water was found the project was abandoned.

My father then decided it would be best to engage a water diviner. A dowser who lived at the village of Croft was recommended to him. An appointment was made. I accompanied my father to meet him and to bring him to Keyham. As we walked from the house up to the site he stopped to cut off a suitable Y-shaped twig from the hedge. Arriving at the site, he walked backwards and forwards around the site where we had been digging with no result. He remarked, 'No water here'.

About 50 yards further on it was a different matter. The twig jumped and swung about and he had a job to hold it. 'Here's your water,' he said, 'a very good supply but I am afraid you will have to dig about 80 feet', and so it proved. The dowser recommended a firm of well-sinkers and they were engaged.

Digging this well proved to be a very costly business but the contractors were professionals. Three men were on the site for about 10 weeks. They did an excellent job and water was found at just over 80 feet. It was customary I understand for the men to celebrate when water is found which they did for the rest of the day at The Dog and Gun. A pump had to be provided; this was a cumbersome affair made of cast iron with a large crank and 4 feet fly wheel. The pump was hand-operated and mounted on the large stone slab. It served its purpose and pumping was good exercise. The water was analysed and reported pure and of excellent quality. A large slab covered the well and as far as I know it still exists.

My father decided it was time to reduce some of the laborious hand work in the fettling shop. To do this more power was required. There was still no chance of an electricity supply coming into the village. A new 10 hp oil engine was ordered from Messrs Richards in Leicester. On its arrival by lorry it was reversed down what was the garden. The driver was asked to help unload but refused saying it was not his job to unload. The engine weighed 30 cwt to 2 tons. We had no lifting tackle in those days. My father told the driver that if he would not help he had better take it back, this spurred him into action. He jumped into his cab and tried to move off. We could see the wheels were sinking in the soft ground; the more he tried the more the wheels sank in. Off came his coat and he worked like a demon with planks and bricks but his efforts were all in vain. The lorry was hopelessly bogged down. With no telephone or means of communication in the village the driver was faced with a walk back to Leicester. My father said he would not see him stranded so he would drive him back to Leicester. The next day Richards sent out a gang of men

The Post Office and village shop, Keyham, *c.* 1914. This small business closed down in 1972, having been run by Miss Gertrude Healey for over 60 years. In 1969 Miss Healey was presented with the BEM for services rendered to the community (see p. 53).

Miss G. Healey, post-mistress and shop keeper at Keyham. Reproduced by kind permission of the *Leicester Mercury*.

to unload the lorry. It was a beautiful-looking engine, the latest design, all moving parts enclosed. I decided that when it was installed I would make it my job to look after it, which I did, although I was still at school.

When my father was working for Russells he was for some years in the iron foundry. This was before he was in charge of the non-ferrous department. During these years he acquired a great deal of knowledge of the production of iron castings. He decided to extend the foundry and make iron castings as well. Using the remaining material left over from the bungalows, a sizeable extension was added. A portion of the building was partitioned off to house the new oil engine. I was pleased about this and begged my father when the engine was installed to put two rows of white tiles round its base. My father had plenty to do without these niceties but after some time he agreed to please me and the tiles were laid, one Sunday morning. I painted 'Engine House' on the door and soon the thing would be ready to go. The shafting had already been installed along the length of the new building to link up with any machines that might be required. The dynamo was moved to its new position to be driven from the new engine. A furnace suitable for melting iron was ordered; this was a Cupalette which was capable of melting iron at the rate of 15 cwt per hour in three or four cwt batches. When the Cupalette arrived at Ingarsby station no lifting facilities were available to unload and there were of course no portable cranes. It was decided that there was no alternative but to take out the inner lining of fire bricks, to make it moveable. Complete it weighed 4 tons. The bricks were removed and the furnace shell loaded on to horse and dray. On arrival at the foundry the furnace had to be relined. It was decided to mount the furnace outside the building. This was not unusual in those days.

A large opening led into the building nearby. Some difficulty was experienced in running the fan at the correct speed. Large pulleys were tried; one of three foot diameter made of wood disintegrated at high speed. Fortunately no one was hurt. Wooden pulleys were in general use then and were built up in sections and glued and screwed together. They were very often made by pattern-makers. It was decided after this to install a metal one, four foot in diameter. This did the trick and provided plenty of air blast, although the extra power taken made the engine cough a bit. The iron came down at record speed and temperatures and when the furnace was started up half the village came to watch. It was night time in the winter; the whine of the engine and the fan and leaping flames out of the top of the furnace caused quite a stir. I think the villagers wondered what Harrisons would do next.

My father had no difficulty in obtaining orders for iron castings and making the moulds was no problem. The greatest difficulty was getting skilled furnace-men to come to Keyham and take charge of the melt. My father carried on for some time doing this himself, casting once a week. Try as he might no suitable person could be found. The project had to be abandoned. My father had more than enough to do managing the non-ferrous side.

Chapter Five

In the Countryside

I must recall some of my experiences and enjoyable times I had as a boy whilst living in Keyham. In the twenties and thirties the countryside was rich in bird-life and as a schoolboy bird-watching became one of my hobbies. I took after my mother who was very knowledgeable about the countryside. When I was quite young she would show me where to look for certain birds' nests. Corncrakes used to breed in the hay meadow at the top of Keyham hill. One could not mistake their 'crake crake crake' as their heads popped up in the mowing grass. This field is now under the plough as it has been for many years. I understand that the only place corncrakes nest now is in the Orkney Islands.

There were many owls, and they bred every year in the trees in the grounds of Keyham Hall. The tawny owl, little owl and barn owl would nest in the holes in the various trees year after year. Cuckoos around the village abounded. I remember one year finding an egg in each of three hedge sparrow's nests, two in our paddock and one in the bullock field. They all hatched out. The constant calling of the cuckoos in the trees around the Top Hall so got on the nerves of the Squire that he instructed his man Harry Wyatt to shoot them, but I don't think he did.

The fields were full of rabbits providing plenty of food for stoats and weasels. It was not unusual to go for a walk in the fields and hear the pitiful cries of a rabbit as it was being stalked by a weasel or stoat and unable to move. One of my pleasures as a boy was to climb the many high hedges to look into magpie nests. Sometimes it would take up to 20 or 30 minutes to have a look inside weaving your way up through the branches breaking off the prickles of the hawthorn branches. Sometimes I would be accompanied by other boys but they would get tired of waiting for me and when I climbed down I would find myself alone. Only persons who have seen inside a magpie's nest can appreciate the skill and beauty of its construction. Only a small hole in one side gains entry. I remember on one occasion while climbing to a nest I had nearly reached the top when a weasel jumped out of the nest slithering down to the ground in a flash; it gave me quite a fright. I wondered whether to proceed to climb or come down. However I had a look inside and there was a very young dead rabbit – presumably it had been taken up there by the weasel.

The railway banks were always a source of interest, as the grasses and many flowers formed good hiding places for birds' nests. One of the less common birds to breed there was the Whinchat. Its nest was cleverly hidden, reached by a tunnel through the grass. Partridges' and pheasants' nests could always be found. Many of the fields had their own ponds, where there were always moorhens breeding. Farmers then depended on these ponds for watering the cattle; now most of the ponds have been filled in, and metal troughs fed from the mains have taken their place.

I was one of a small party of boys following the brook which went past the Jarroms' farm and on over the Beeby road. Kingfishers were attracted by the high banks to bore holes for their nests and deep pools adjacent to provide fish for their young. I saw a kingfisher fly out of its nesting hole in a steep bank; this was too good a chance to miss. A small boy who was with us at the time was persuaded to be lowered down the bank head first with two of us holding his legs. He put his small arm up the hole where there were several eggs. He held one for us to see, it was a beautiful, nearly round glossy egg. The egg was returned to the nest which was made almost entirely of fish bones: a slimy, stinking mess. You can imagine the boy needed a good wash in the brook, before returning home.

Arriving late in April or early May nightingales would take up their residence in Scraptoft Woods in Covert Lane, sometimes as many as three could be heard singing in the daytime as well as at night. With all the other birds singing in the daytime it was not always possible to distinguish them from the other birds. I would sometimes crawl very quietly under the bushes in daylight where one was singing until looking up I could watch the movements of its throat. Its nest I searched for in vain until years later during 1939, I was walking along Ingarsby Road where there was a spinney on the right hand side. I was surprised to hear a nightingale singing in a tree. I entered the spinney searching for a possible nest with no luck. A few weeks later I once more entered the spinney to have a final look and just inside in a low bush was its nest. There were four young birds – what a thrill. I bent down to have a closer look and they all fluttered out as they were ready to fly. They quickly dispersed in the undergrowth. One of the parent birds emitted its croaking note in alarm. There was one infertile egg still in the nest. This was the nearest I have heard of a nightingale visiting Keyham. I have heard it said that they could be heard singing in bushes on Keyham Hill at the turn of the century. Many birds would nest in the low bushes around the Hill, particularly migratory birds, blackcaps, garden warblers, chiff-chaffs, white-throats, and willow warblers. Yellowhammers would nest in the banks of the ditches nearby.

I had a friend, Mr Morley, who owned the Provincial Garage on Uppingham Road. He was one of the first to run licensed buses to the seaside resorts in the 1930s. He would arrange evening trips in the summer around the country villages. I told him about the nightingales in the woods at Scraptoft. One evening he put a noticeboard outside his garage stating 'A trip to hear the nightingales 1/6'. He had no difficulty in getting a full bus load. Instead of driving straight to the wood he would take his passengers on a roundabout trip until it was getting dark. This disguised his route. I walked up to the fields to wait his arrival. Sure enough to the delight of his passengers three nightingales could be heard singing.

In 1922 I was 14 years old and my school days were over. I was not sorry that my time to start work had arrived, as I had already spent a good deal of time in the foundry and was acquainted with the men. My wages were 4/- per week and my keep of course. My father insisted I joined the building society; he paid the first premium of 2s per week. This was the Leicester Temperance Building Society whose office was in Belvoir St., Leicester. I never faltered with the payments and this amounted with interest to about £105 in 1956 when I drew it out to purchase some accessories to equip a caravan which I had purchased. I used to sit on a bench watching the moulders. They were very helpful and eventually I was able to make moulds of simple things which were cast and sold to customers. I was always good at handwork at school and often top of the class. Foundrywork requires a great deal of skill with the hands and a very gentle touch. I acquired all these faculties which were necessary as there was little machinery available. Today things are very different; much of the skill has been taken out of moulding by the use of special sands bonded with chemicals.

My wages increased to 8/- per week and my brother Robert was paid the same when he started work in 1924. I continued to be responsible for looking after the oil engine as I had for a year or two before I left school. If it needed mechanical attention my Uncle Fred and his wife Nellie would be invited to come over on a Sunday. My Uncle Fred was a fitter and worked for Russells. The wear in the big end would require adjusting by the removal of steel shims.

Uncle Fred asked me to start the engine so he could listen to it running. After about five minutes it was stopped, and he unscrewed the wing nut which removed the end plate to get at the big end. The big end connecting rod was totally enclosed in a one piece casting. It really was a beautifully designed engine. Fred said, 'It's dark in here, can you get me a candle?' I fetched him a candle and I was craning my head near his, eager to look inside, when he struck a match to light it. There was a loud explosion as the unburnt gas in the chamber exploded. We were kneeling down at the time and both were blown over backwards. Neither of us were hurt except for scorched eyebrows and eyelashes. My Uncle was a bit dazed and said he could do with a glass of beer.

When we arrived in the house my Aunt Nellie, who was highly emotional, said 'What ever have you been doing Fred: you look as though you have seen a ghost, look at your eyebrows and eyelashes'. Fred said, 'We have made a brief trip to hell'. She rounded on my father saying 'Bert, what have you been getting him to do?' On future occasions when the big end required attention I was able to attend to it myself.

Although the foundry at Keyham was to some degree successful enabling us all to earn a living, there were many times, isolated in a village with no telephone, my father missed out on orders. Some of his customers would say 'Bob, we can't find you when we want you'. He realised something ought to be done. A small foundry was for sale in Causeway Lane, Leicester and when my father heard about this he became interested. It had been a long-alley skittle alley originally and probably belonged at some time to the Bishop Blaze pub next door. It had been nicely fitted out as a brass foundry. There were four coke-fired pit furnaces, and gas lighting. There was no power or telephone but these were added later. The site included 14 houses, all slum property and condemned. The conditions there were terrible. There was a courtyard in which the children played. They called it the field, but not a single blade of grass grew there.

The estate, known as 'Bishops' Terrace' had a covered alley-way entrance. This was five foot wide and had about three families living over it; a cobbler still in business, a slaughterman and a Salvation Army woman. The 'Sally' would visit all the local public houses each week to sell a copy of the *War Cry*, including one to the foundry.

The foundry entrance was down the alleyway through a door at the side and was only wide enough for a wheelbarrow or small truck. The asking price was £1600. My father paid a visit to his bank, the Midland, borrowed the £1600 and bought the property. This acquisition, during 1919, proved to be very convenient providing him with a central office where he could always be found each day between 12 and 2. It was also a convenience that customers could obtain a casting quickly for breakdown jobs. One man and a youth apprentice were employed there.

Residents of Keyham made good use of the new business. If they had a big parcel they would leave it there and my father would arrange for it to be delivered to Keyham. Miss Healey, who ran Keyham Post Office and shop, would arrange for most of her goods to be delivered there as her suppliers would not deliver to Keyham. My father would charge 2d per parcel or perhaps 4d for a larger one, such as a large parcel of cigarettes. My brother and I or my sisters would deliver them to the post office. We were always rewarded with a few sweets or a bar of chocolate.

Bill Lester, who was the first to join my father at Keyham, lodged at the farm next door with Mr and Mrs Jack Sanderson. Bill was a widower and after the Freer family came to live at The Nether Hall he became friendly with the lady who was the cook. This friendship developed and they decided to marry. It was arranged that Bill should go to Leicester to manage the foundry at Causeway Lane. To do this he obtained a house in Tudor Road, Leicester. Towards the end of World War One, Mrs Lester joined him to work in the foundry for a short time. She soon became an efficient bench moulder. Bill, apart from being a skilled moulder, used to melt his own metal and cast his moulds. A 60 lb crucible was used, this being about the right size for the type of work being made at that time.

Foundrymen of those days often wore moleskin trousers to come to work. Bill Lester was no exception. They were particularly suitable for moulders or foundry workers, especially those working on the benches, because of their hard-wearing qualities. Although called moleskins they had no connection with moles although the cloth did resemble a mole, being brushed cotton. The fabric was closely woven thick cotton. This thick material provided some protection against splashes of molten metal. Their only fault however was their smell when brand new. When I was 18 I wore moleskin trousers. I felt quite a foundryman and grown up with my moulder's trowel sticking out of my hip pocket.

Causeway Lane being so convenient enabled my father to build up a small scrap metal business. It was amazing what articles were melted down; pewter mugs, teapots and plates, all kinds of articles in brass and pewter including beautiful brass chandeliers. No one seemed interested in objects of art in those days, but today this scrap would be worth a fortune.

Mr Lester carried on managing the Causeway Lane foundry until 1923; the Lesters' daughter, Mary, was born in 1919 in Leicester. It so happened that one of the bungalows on the hill became available and Mr Lester and family decided to occupy this and to come and live in Keyham. This move into the village meant he had to travel back and forth to work each day to Causeway Lane, including Saturday. His daily routine would consist of walking to the Humberstone tram terminus, as it was known in those days, near Humberstone park, then catching a tram from there to the Clock Tower, and then he had a quarter of an hour's walk to Causeway Lane arriving at 7.30am. On the return journey he would walk to the Haymarket and catch Toons bus back to Scraptoft and walk home from there. This he did in all weathers. On Saturday he would drive back with my father on the back of the lorry. This he did for many years until at the age of 65 in 1936 he retired. Looking back I have often marvelled at Bill's tenacity and willingness for hard work and loyalty to my father. In fact this loyalty to my father applied to all his employees. I can remember sometimes after my father had paid his men's wages there was little left.

It was usual for my father to purchase back from his customers the turnings and drillings which came off the brass castings during machining. These often contained particles of iron. This came about when the machine operator had to change over to machining parts of iron or steel and the turnings became mixed. These had to be removed and a hand-operated magnetic filtering machine was purchased. This provided my brother and I with pocket money when we were at school. It was our job to fill up the hopper on the machine and turn the handle slowly. The iron separated from the brass, the iron falling in a tray at the rear and the brass into a large bucket at the front of the machine. We were paid three pence for a bucket full which would usually take about twenty minutes. It was a boring daily job. We would race one another after school to be first to get the job done. Until this job was finished, the metal could not be melted down. It was sometimes weeks before the batch was through, and then there was a break until the next lot. My father never gave us pocket money but would always find us something useful to do for which we were paid. I am sure this taught us the value of money.

My father engaged a property agent to collect the rents from the fourteen houses. The occupants nearly all had big families and were very poor. The rents were a few shillings a week. An unlicensed bookie whose name was Bill Blower occupied one of the houses. There was a regular stream of punters up and down the passageway especially on big race days. No doubt this is where some of the rent money went.

By now the 10 cwt Ford Van was getting the worse for wear and it was decided to dispense with it. My father saw an advertisement in the Leicester Mercury advertising redundant Ford Post Office vans. He bought three of these for the sum of £12. All were more or less in running order and had Royal Mail painted in big letters on the side. He was able to sell two of these for £12 and decided to keep one to use in place of the van. It was in regular use for two or three years. The Royal Mail sign had to be painted out and some of his customers were quite amused when he was delivering castings and would make fun: 'Here's Bob with the Royal Mail'.

As there was no public transport into Leicester we children had to provide our own entertainment in the village. I decided with others to form a boys' cricket team. The Squire allowed us the free use of a section of the men's cricket field. We soon had a pitch rolled and mown using the men's roller and hand mower. We played matches with other local villages, Hungarton, Houghton on the Hill, Scraptoft etc. Our pitch unfortunately was rather near to the brook. Mr Hincks came down to watch one day, and realising our difficulty kindly promised to send us a roll of wire netting to fence the brook boundary. This arrived in due course including some cricketing equipment, bats, pads etc, that he had used in his young days.

We young people in the village were very lucky being allowed the run of all the fields. Brook jumping was a very popular pastime, also spinning tops and bowling, with motor tyres.

The foundry yard was always a source of interest; one never knew what my father would bring home next. One day he came home with two old muzzle-loaded guns with fluted barrels. They were separated from the stocks but it was not long before two of the boys in the village found out how to fix them together. When my father, coming out of the foundry saw what was happening, they were having great fun pointing them at one another. I think he could see the possible danger and took possession of the two guns and threw them onto a coke fire in a core oven where cores were being dried. After a few seconds there was a loud explosion, the core oven door was blown open and all the cores broken. Apparently there was a live charge in one of the barrels. Those old muzzle-loaders would be valuable antiques today.

The village shop and post office played an important part in the lives of the residents of Keyham. It was occupied by Mrs Healey 'an aged lady' and her daughter Gertrude, better known to the villagers as Gerty. As a girl she was learning dressmaking in Leicester and travelled there and back each day on her cycle. Her mother looked after the shop selling sweets; rows of glass jars on the counter contained boiled sweets of all kinds. On the wall behind was a hook containing squares of newspaper. Mrs Healey was adept at forming a cornet-shaped bag to hold the boiled sweets, just a quick twist of her fingers and then on the scales. Sometimes if she was offered a coin worn or bent she would drop it on the stone floor to see if it had the right ring or sound. Mrs Healey was quite a small person and always wore a lace bonnet behind the counter.

At the age of 21 Gerty applied for Keyham to have its own Post Office, and she became the subpostmistress during 1912. A post box was let flush in the wall to the right of the shop window. From then on Keyham shop gradually became a village store, and was licensed to sell tobacco. Most of the residents were able to obtain their food requirements and such diverse items as paraffin, mouse traps, firelighters etc. Paraffin was only available after 6pm. I think Gerty must have taken after her mother because many years later when my young daughter tendered a shilling to buy something (the coin may have looked a bit old) she put it between her teeth to bite it and said, 'Is this one your father made in the foundry?' Maureen came home very upset and said she would never go into the shop again.

The post office was the first property to have a telephone installed. One or two of our customers who were given the number, would sometimes phone if the matter was urgent. Gerty would get on her cycle, lock the shop door and ride down to tell us we were wanted on the 'phone. Robert or I would dash up on our motor bikes to take the call. This went on until we were able to have our own phone installed.

When Gerty Healey retired after sixty years service (for which she received the B.E.M.) the shop closed, and was converted to a private dwelling in about 1978. The old smithy next to the shop was converted into a garage for the house.

During 1920 my father decided to think of the family's social needs. He had been working long hours for many years and had not had a holiday for 18 years. My mother was also keen to have our own transport to enable her and the children to visit her family at Woodford. My father had ordered a new Model T Ford touring car, some months before. This had now arrived much to our excitement. This car cost the magnificent sum of £120. Apart from the need for family outings the car was important in following-up business inquiries.

Occasionally my father and Jeffson would travel to Newark together, both to conduct their respective business. This would be in my father's Model T Ford Tourer. Sometimes I was allowed to go with them. I would sit in the rear seat and had to sit there until their business was finished. On the return journey we would call at a pub about 8 miles from Newark for about an hour. I was about 13 at the time. Jeffson would order my father a pint of beer, I had a bottle of lemonade and he himself would have a double scotch with milk. He would have about three of these before we started for home. This did not seem to have any ill effect on him. I remember once on a similar journey, we were bowling along at a good pace, about 40 to 45 miles per hour. This was the car's maximum speed. Suddenly some smoke appeared and Jeffson cried out, 'I am on fire, stop, I'm on fire'. A wad of burning tobacco had fallen from my father's pipe which he was smoking at the time and fell in Jeffson's lap and set his trousers alight. My father quickly stopped the car and Jeffson said 'You bugger – you're not satisfied with trying to break my neck; you want to set fire to me as well'.

The holiday season was approaching and it was decided to go for a week's holiday to Skegness. It was August bank holiday. When we arrived in the new car all the boarding houses seemed to be full up and we could not get accommodation. There were seven of us in all. We were told that a few miles outside the town we would be able to find accommodation. We returned about eight miles to a village called Friskney, where a noticeboard said one mile to the sea. When we got there, the sea was barely visible in the distance, and it was just a desolate waste of marshland pitted with ridges and water-filled holes. A noticeboard warned visitors not to try and walk out to the sea because of the danger of fast incoming tides. We turned round and on the way back to the main road we called at a fisherman's cottage. They were willing to provide us with accommodation for three. My father, brother and myself decided to stay here. They very kindly suggested that they had other relations who lived further down the road who might be able to help us to fix up the rest of the family. They agreed and my mother stayed there with my sisters. We were all provided with breakfast, after which we spent the rest of the day in Skegness. We were made very comfortable and enjoyed our stay. On our departure it came as a surprise when both families wanted to adopt two of us. The fisherman wanted to adopt my brother Robert and the other family who were farmers wanted to adopt my sister Cissie. Neither family had any children of their own and they had never seen such well-behaved children. My mother's reply after thanking them sincerely was that she would rather have more than part with one of us. What a tribute to my parents.

As more and more new cars came onto the market, scrap dealers were buying the old ones. My father became interested because of the large amount of brass and copper they contained. Our yard became full of these old cars, quite like a museum. Some of them would have qualified as Brighton runners today. There was the De Dion Bouton, a Renault, a beautiful Daimler Saloon, a Swift and many others. My brother and I had the time of our lives, after school and at weekends. Some of the cars were able to be driven, and we would get the engines going. The Swift had an all-chain drive to the rear wheels. It had at the rear what was known as a sprag, connected to it was a leather strap which led to the driver's seat. If the car got stuck on a hill, the driver would release the strap, the sprag would drop and stick in the ground preventing the car from running backwards. Brakes were not very efficient in those days. The Swift was our favourite. We took the engine out to make it lighter and went out with it on the road pushing it up hills and free-wheeling down. We gave rides to the village boys and girls. It was with this that my brother and I learnt to steer. These old cars would be bought at prices of between £4 and £10 each. Many stayed in the yard for years before being taken to pieces to recover the non-ferrous scrap.

A Mr and Mrs Hadfield who had no children came from Sheffield to occupy the White House Farm at Keyham. Mr Hadfield was a representative for Wards of Sheffield. They were big suppliers to the Foundry trade. During the course of his travels he would visit my father for orders. As a result they took a liking to Keyham village and during the latter half of the 1920s they came and settled there. They stayed for a number of years. They were a very friendly couple, always ready and willing to help anyone in the village. I remember they had a small car – I cannot remember the make – perhaps it was a one-off. It was a two seater with an air cooled V-shaped 2 cylinder Jap engine. This was mounted at the front. It had no gear box or clutch. Its transmission was known as a friction drive. This consisted of two steel discs which were controlled by a lever giving two forward speeds, neutral and reverse. We young men in our early teens were intrigued by this. We would go on Sunday mornings up to the shed at the rear of the house where it was kept. A Mr McFoden, some relation to the Hadfield family, would come over from Leicester on Sunday mornings on his motor cycle. I think he was a motor mechanic and he would explain to us all the workings. He really was a know-all. We would gather round hoping he would start the engine and take it for a spin. This he did from time to time down the Ingarsby Road. Cap on back to front he would disappear with a bang and a splutter. We would follow behind sometimes helping him to push it back. I understand it arrived from Sheffield to Keyham under its own power with Mac at the wheel.

I remember Robert taking out one of the veteran cars from the foundry yard accompanied by other boys. This car was chain driven to the back axle. We would push it up the hills past the post office and then free-wheel down for the ride. On this occasion Mr Hadfield, who was walking up the village street and seeing we were struggling, offered to give us a push. Unfortunately as he was leaning forward, his very nice navy blue overcoat got caught in the oily chain sprocket and we had to reverse the car to free it. Naturally he was not very pleased. I think we all managed to keep a straight face at the time but we certainly had a laugh afterwards.

In the early twenties the age of radio had arrived. One day whilst in Leicester I visited Woolworths and noticed they were selling radio crystals; they were 6d each and mounted in a small brass cup. A friend living in the village, Leslie Francis, suggested we should try to make a crystal set. We had plenty of copper wire in the foundry. Unfortunately this was bare copper, no insulation covering. We soon got over this however: we stretched a length of it across the yard and painted it with enamel. We found some square brass rods to make a tuner and some copper wire to make a cat's whisker. An old hand telephone receiver was used for headphones. We now had all the ingredients but lacked the know-how. Needless to say this first attempt did not work. It was not until the Nottingham relay station opened that crystal sets became a proposition in Keyham. We persevered and as components came available we were successful. We fixed a high aerial above the foundry roof. This proved to be our greatest asset. From this we had good reception on headphones with crystal sets. Miss Hincks at the Top Hall had a magnificent 5 valve receiver in a cabinet. This was supplied and manufactured by Gents of Leicester and was battery operated. At the Top Hall they had loud-speakers wired in most of the downstairs rooms. My mother noticed my interest in radio and came back from Leicester one day with a 3 valve receiver, new but unwired. It had no valves, and no batteries. She had seen it in the window of Youngs the Chemist in Belvoir Street, price £4.10.0d. I was thrilled with this but doubtful whether I would be able to wire it and get it to go. There was a small wiring diagram but no other instructions whatever. I obtained some square tinned copper wire and a tin of fluxite. The soldering iron was an old one from the foundry with a 1 lb copper bit. My soldering efforts consisted of dropping blobs of solder onto the wires that were to be joined together. My mother suggested I took it back to Youngs and ask their advice. Fortunately Mr Young had his nephew staying with him; the nephew was a university student taking an electronics course. He agreed to return home with me and help with the wiring. My mother had lit the fire in the front room to heat the iron. He settled down and told me to strip off all the wiring and bring him a fire brick, which was placed in the hearth. He then showed me how to tin the soldering iron. This was the secret of soldering and something I had never heard of. He proceeded to solder and wire the set. I felt that I had really learnt something. My mother provided him with tea and he said he would have to be getting back. The wiring was three parts finished and I felt confident that I could complete the rest. I asked him if he would wire up the LF transformer before he went as this had the four wires protruding out of the transformer and no terminals or markings. I accompanied him back on the lorry, being very grateful for his help. The set was completed some time later. Three cosser valves were purchased for 12/6 each, and a 66 volt HT battery. I already had a 6v accumulator from one of the cars. The set worked perfectly and provided us with much entertainment using headphones for a number of years. This encouragement by my mother and the help of my friend from Youngs made me decide to take up amateur radio as a hobby.

In the early '20s there were several licensed radio amateurs in the district. I used to listen to these on Sunday mornings. They were allowed to use the broadcast bands until 12pm. This was when the BBC started to come on the air. One radio amateur was Henry Field, son by her first marriage of Mrs Burnaby at Baggrave Hall. He invited me to bring a small party over to the hall to see his equipment. It was Christmas Eve. There were about four of us in the party, Tom Harris from the Nether Hall, my brother Robert, Clarrie and myself. We cycled over. It was a bright moonlit frosty night and as we rode through the Baggrave Park we could hear a loudspeaker blasting away.

This loudspeaker was situated at an open window upstairs in the billiard room which he used for his radio experiments. He had everything: a low-powered transmitter for local work and a high-powered transmitter for transatlantic work. This had two large round valves screened off in a wire cage. There was radio apparatus of all kinds. There were others in the party, or rather others in the room, who had also been invited for the evening.

When we arrived at about 7.30 he explained his apparatus and the records he held for long-distance transmitting. He then disappeared leaving us with the loudspeakers blaring away. He reappeared in about two hours in evening dress smoking a cigar. We began to wonder if it was likely that there would be any refreshments as it was Christmas Eve. We stayed until about 12 o'clock and then took our leave. So much for upper class hospitality, not even a mince pie.

Trying to run a village cricket team was very difficult as many of the farm labourers were unable to play on Saturday afternoons because of their milking duties. The village cricket pitch was situated in the field below the village, bordered by the brook on one side and the hedge on the other side of Snows Lane. The rising bank on the hedge side made an ideal grandstand for spectators. The boys would sit on the bank on the other side of the brook so that they could retrieve the ball and throw it to the nearest fielder. The playing pitch had of course to be fenced in by a detachable posts let in concrete sockets. To these were added three strands of barbed wire. The posts and wire were lifted out and removed to the outfield during matches. This fencing was necessary because cows and bullocks regularly occupied the field but were taken out during the match days. The brook was a bit of a hazard – it was known for a player in the outfield, while running with his head in the air to catch a ball, to fall in the water. Another hazard was when the ball landed in a freshly laid cow-pat. This usually meant an extra run or two while it was retrieved. The team would retire to The Dog and Gun for the interval, tea being prepared by the landlord.

The Baxter family who had lived at the Top Hall prior to 1914, had decided to leave the village. However, their son Major Joe Baxter and his mother came back to live at Keyham in 1922, occupying the thatched cottage, after Joe's war service. He was instrumental in forming the village cricket team and was elected Captain. The team was very successful for a number of years and Joe was a good bowler. However, after some years

Joe and his mother left the village. The Captaincy of the cricket team was then taken over by Joe Taylor. Joe was one of the Taylor family who occupied Glebe Farm. There were seven in the family – five girls and two boys. The house and buildings have now been demolished. It was situated in the fields between Ingarsby and Keyham. Joe worked for his father on the farm. His brother William was killed during World War One. I am told there was great resentment in the village subsequently, when his younger brother Joseph was called up for active service although he was only eighteen years old at the time. There were other men in the village who were eligible for active service but not called up.

Mr Tunnicliffe, Ernie as he was known by all the patrons of the Dog and Gun, was employed by my father part-time. Some of the windows from the foundry overlooked the pub yard and when the beer lorry arrived Ernie would lower one of the windows and climb out to attend to it.

He also kept bees, and in the summer sometimes they would swarm in our garden. Ernie never used to protect himself against stings. He used to get stung horribly on his face and did not seem to mind.

At the rear of the Dog and Gun was a large elm tree, and under this there was a long alley skittle pitch. From the windows of the foundry we could watch the play. Old man Randle had the job of fetching the beer for the players. He walked with a limp and a stick and while just out of sight of the players he would take a sup from each glass. Mr Randle ran a smallholding at Keyham during his younger days but unfortunately met with a serious accident while hedge cutting and lost the sight of an eye.

The old post office van had done its bit. After two years of continuous use it was worn out and often had difficulty in getting up Keyham Hill when it was fully loaded. It finally took its place in the yard with the other scrap vehicles, and was replaced by a brand new one ton Ford Model T Lorry, registration number NR 622. This was a big step forward. More and more materials had to be carried backwards and forwards. The customers would say 'Bob's coming on, he's got a brand new lorry'.

I would sometimes accompany my father with a load of castings to Newark. This was during the early Twenties and on one occasion we had two burst tyres although they were brand new. I remember my father saying, 'That's put paid to the profit on this lot'. We had to stay the night at Newark and my father had to send a telegram to my mother acquainting her with what had happened. We stayed the night at the Temperance Hotel.

This change of transport did not deter people from the village: they were still very glad to have a ride to Leicester. My father fixed some seats in the back of the lorry and dropped down one side to help them mount. There did not appear to be anything unusual in riding on the back of a lorry.

It was soon after purchasing the lorry that my father came home with an old church bier. I suppose it was brought to Causeway Lane by one of the metal dealers. If he had known the outcome I am sure he would have left it alone. It was very old but in perfect condition. It had no tyres, just metal rims on the wheels. It must have been made before tyres were invented. My brother and I were soon testing its merits out on the road with the other boys and girls in the village. We would push it up hills and free-wheel down Snows Lane and the hill near Miss Healey's shop. There were no brakes but it was easy to steer by the feet of the one sitting on the front. Miss Healey used to say 'I know they will be through my window one of these days'. The iron rimmed wheels made a great clatter; all this added to the fun. This went on for some time. It should be remembered that we had the road all to ourselves then, except perhaps for the odd horse and cart.

It happened one day that my father was stranded on Keyham Hill. There was nothing unusual about this. It was very steep and had a distinct dip near the centre. (This was eventually filled in.) My mother heard of my father's plight and told us boys to go to see if we could help. Off we went taking the bier with us, accompanied by Jimmy Archer and another boy who was with us. Pushing the bier and riding along the level we arrived at Keyham Hill. There was my father with his lorry half way down well on his proper side. Jimmy was sitting on the front in the steering position. We stopped at the top and I said we were not riding down as it was too steep and dangerous. Jimmy, daring as ever, spotted a piece of wooden railing in the hedge. He wedged this across the bier so that one end pressed on one of the wheels acting as a brake. The other boy was sitting on the back. I would not get on: I was always cautious when danger threatened. Away they went before I could stop them. They had only gone about 15 yards before the piece of wood snapped. The bier was gathering speed all the time, but just before it was level my father leapt out meeting it head on. He leaned forward and with superhuman strength forced it to a standstill, having been pushed back at least 25 yards. It was a most courageous thing to do. He could easily have been injured. I was frightened. When I arrived on the scene, I received a good telling off for bringing the thing. Jimmy had already had his ears boxed. My father was naturally furious. We were ordered to take it back immediately and put it in the yard. The next day it was destroyed with a sledge-hammer.

It was the usual practice in Keyham on New Year's Eve to ring the old year out and the new year in on the church bells. But the year 1919 was to be an exception. Mr Hincks had settled in the village and in view of the changes he was making Teddy Johnson, who was one of the church wardens, did not want to give the impression that Mr Hincks was being welcomed in the village. The church was always locked in those days. He realised the lads of the village might get the key from Mr Randle who was the key holder and ring the bells as usual. He therefore made sure he got possession of the key. The young men in the village were very disappointed, Clarrie amongst them. It was usual for them to ring a muffled peel on the bells for ringing the old year out and then remove the muffles on the stroke of twelve to ring in the new year.

I had been sworn to secrecy by Norman, my friend and Teddy's son, but when I told my father about the plan, he had other ideas. He arranged with my mother to hold a party and celebrate the new year. There was a large bell in the foundry, which was hung on a beam. My father hit this with a hammer – in fact, we were all equipped with hammers. There were about 8 or 10 in the party. The idea was to create as much noise as possible. There were plenty of noise-producing articles in the foundry including old coppers. Some of these were taken out in the yard and turned upside down and hit with hammers. This sounded like tom-toms. At the stroke of Midnight we kicked up a terrible din. The noise woke some of the neighbours who came out to see what was going on. They were annoyed but when they saw there was plenty of beer flowing, bread and cheese and my mother's mince pies they soon joined in the fun and we kept the party going until the early hours. I never heard if the Squire heard the noise but Norman my friend did, and he blamed me for not keeping his secret.

When the four bungalows built by my father were completed, there was a considerable quantity of building material left over, roof trusses, timber and corrugated iron etc. This was removed to the half paddock retained by my father at the rear of The White House. This soon became overgrown with long grass and beds of nettles. The Guinea fowl next door soon found this to their liking. Mrs Woodford couldn't understand why she wasn't getting any eggs, but guinea fowl are notorious for laying their eggs away. When she found out what was happening she wasn't very pleased. After this the fowl were kept in a wire enclosure. When Mr and Mrs Woodford died my father had the opportunity of buying back the piece of land from their executors for £25, therefore once more owning the whole of the paddock. When Mr Hincks heard of this he was very cross; he had not heard it was for sale and did not like anyone owning land in his village.

In the year 1924 Keyham could at last say it was on the map. A daily bus service was inaugurated from Leicester Haymarket to Hungarton calling at Keyham. The bus was an ex-army Model T Ford. The bus body could be taken off and a lorry body substituted if required, and it was driven by its owner, a Mr Arthur Norledge and nicknamed 'The Bed Tick'. It had open sides with blinds that could be put down if it rained and rolled up if it was fine. The blinds were made of bed ticking, hence the nickname. It was recorded in the local press that his first order came from a Hungarton lady who asked him to transport a half ounce of snuff, a Leicester Mercury and half a pound of tomatoes. This bus service proved very popular. Some years later Arthur decided to expand his services. It sometimes happened that at weekends the bus was full and some passengers had to be left behind. A much smaller second-hand bus was acquired, also a Model T Ford. It was a neat little bus that carried about 6 or 8 passengers. A young man called George, a farm labourer who lived in the village, was approached as he wanted to learn to drive, and he decided to join forces with Mr Norledge. He invested his savings of £100 and the extra services were commenced. This went well until one day when George was driving the small bus with a full load of passengers. It was a Saturday and as it arrived at Keyham and turned to go down Snows Lane, one of the passengers called out 'Stop, I want to get out here'. George slammed on his brakes to stop and the brakes failed. The back axle or half shaft had broken, and when this happens the brakes are useless on a Model T Ford. He called out 'The brakes have gone, the brakes have gone' which caused panic. I was in the garage of The White House at the time with the doors open and when the bus rushed by with the passengers screaming, it must have been travelling at 50 mph. As it disappeared in a cloud of dust two of the passengers jumped out near Pear Tree Farm. They were badly bruised and cut but not seriously injured. The bus carried on completely out of control, crashing through the hedge and turned upside-down in the cricket field. I was first at the scene. I wrenched open the doors and helped get the passengers out. They were very shocked and bruised but otherwise not seriously injured. Handbags, groceries, shopping and loose change were everywhere. I was worried because of petrol leaking from the vent in the petrol filler cap. The petrol tank was under the driver's seat in those days. Poor George the driver did not know where he was, he seemed to be in a trance. Mrs Sanderson, one of the passengers, soon recovered and with the help of her family got the kettle going and made tea for everyone. She was living at Pear Tree Farm at the time. Mrs Walker, another one of the passengers, was pregnant at the time but suffered no bad effects. With hindsight the driver should have steered the bus into the earth bank as soon as the brakes failed, and this would have quickly slowed up the vehicle bringing it to a standstill. Instead he steered it down the centre of the road and down the hill, gathering speed all the time. The bus was a complete write-off. One rear wheel came off as it overturned and was found near the brook with part of the broken axle attached.

My father had a similar experience when crossing the Clock Tower. The axle snapped and the wheel came off and careered across the clock tower. It was retrieved by a policeman on point duty, who on bringing it back said 'Is this yours?'.

The Bed Tick

Alas the bed-tick is no more
It started life 'round Twenty-four
And more or less could carry a score.

Its wooden body plain and strong
Weathered the storms as it went along.
We climbed four steps to reach its deck

And paid our sixpence on the step.
With one on the front to open the gates
We started off in fine estate.

It had solid tyres in its earliest days
But these proved too bumpy for Keyham's highways,
Its open sides when breezes blew
Worried us not as night-time drew.
Its bench type seats we did not mind
We sat in the dark and pulled down the blinds.

The blinds when unfurled were a pretty sight,
They were made of bed-ticking
And kept out the light.
And that's how its nick-name first came to be,
But please do not think it was christened by me.
The owner driver, a kindly man
Would often oblige a passenger fan
And stop on the way for a paper to buy,
Or last minute shopping
He would never say nay.
Its time-keeping schedules need I say went awry
And sometimes its passengers had to walk all the way.

Its greatest test was Keyham Hill
Where we all got out and pushed with a will.
Its patrons now are few and far,
But those still left must shed a tear
When they think of the days of yester year.
For bed-tick days have now gone by
and Midland Red can't satisfy.
So all that's left for us to mourn
Are distant memories of Keyham's FIRST BUS
                              Rowles Harrison

The Timson family who occupied Mayfield Farm decided to give up farming after receiving notice to quit. A sale was arranged to dispose of their stock and farm implements. Mr Timson, a retired builder, bought some land at Covert Lane, Scraptoft, to build a house. Two or three rooms were quickly built and occupied by part of the family. This included Mr and Mrs Timson, Clarrie, Roy and Connie. It had a flat roof. The building of it was a long term effort due to financial difficulties and it was some years before it was completed. It was named Quorn Villa. This change of abode meant that Clarrie with a crippled foot had a one mile walk morning and night to and from his work at the foundry. Clarrie never grumbled and was always on time,

Eric Purple and Jack
Hargreaves fixing new
weathercock at All
Saints Church,
Keyham, March 1984.

except on one occasion when the brook was flooded after very long and
heavy rain. There was a foot of water over the footbridge which he had
to cross. Someone came to tell us 'Your man can't get across the floods'.
I went down to the stile and Clarrie called out and waved his crutch.
We managed to get him across with the help of some waders. Clarrie
was keen on shooting and bought a new BSA Point 22 rifle. He obtained
a permit for its use and brought it to work. On his way home he would
shoot a rabbit. Many years later I was asked to cast a new weathercock
for the village church. This was presented to the church by Mrs

Mrs F. Staunton and the author with the weathercock outside the foundry in Gough Rd., Leicester.

Staunton of Nether Hall. When I examined the old one I found a small bullet hole right through the copper shell. I couldn't help thinking who might have been responsible.

As a matter of interest I would like to record that the present new weathercock is made of cast aluminium, using the old one as a pattern after much reconditioning. It was anodised to give it a golden colour and protection from the elements.

Clarrie would sometimes go in the woods on a moonlit night and shoot pheasants with a twelve-bore gun. My brother Robert and I decided to accept his invitation to join him one evening, so off we went. I had a catapult, my brother his air rifle and we joined Clarrie. The house was at the edge of a spinney and it was a beautiful moonlit night, sticks crackling under foot. I was on edge in case we were caught. We did not tell our parents what we were up to. Pheasants roost some 10 to 20 feet up often in old magpies' nests. We wandered about for half an hour. Suddenly we heard one chatter overhead. It was about 20 feet up and we could see it plainly in the moonlight. Clarrie was quick on the draw and down it fell, but it lodged on a branch about ten foot up, and was squawking loudly. I tried to dislodge it with my catapult but with no success. Clarrie reached up with his crutch and brought it down and soon wrung its neck. We started for home soon afterwards with the pheasant under my coat. When we arrived safely indoors there was a sudden knock at the door. We quickly put the pheasant under the table. We thought we had been followed but it was a false alarm. This escapade was not repeated after a strict warning from my father.

Tom Timson, the eldest son of the Timson family and Clarrie's brother, apparently showed distinct musical talent very early on. His mother arranged for him to have piano lessons. He made rapid progress and at the age of six it was said he gave a performance in front of Queen Victoria. During the First World War Tom joined up as a soldier. After his demob in 1918 his services as a pianist were in great demand at Keyham dances. He charged 10s to play from 8pm–12pm. The dances were held in the school room using the school piano. Tom could play all the old dances including the Lancers, without the aid of music. After the last dance sometimes we would ask him to render his own composition of the loss of the *Titanic*. It was very realistic, ending with 'Nearer my God to thee'. This sent cold shudders down our backs.

Tom never made good use of his talent and adopted a come-day-go-day attitude. He sometimes played the piano in the Dog and Gun at weekends for a sing song. He worked for the squire as a farm labourer and occupied one of his cottages in the village. This did not last and he then moved to a small wooden bungalow in Covert Lane near his father's house. He later had a family of four, including twins. They had to walk down the fields to the school in Keyham. Little Tommy aged five and his sister Dorothy two years older would arrive at school sometimes on a cold winter's morning ill-clad and crying with the cold. It was pitiful to see them blue with cold. Miss Sharpe had to thaw them out before lessons commenced.

There was a wedding in the village. Clarrie Timson was to be married to Tom Buswell's daughter Gertrude. He had been courting her for more than a year. Clarrie had always been popular with the girls, because of his good looks and cheerful disposition. One of his brothers acted as Best Man and Tom gave his daughter away. After the wedding Clarrie and his bride drove round to their newly built family house, Quorn Villa in Covert Lane, in his father's horse and float. It was a beautiful sunny day and the other members and guests of the wedding decided after a visit to the Dog and Gun they would walk up the fields following the footpath. Unfortunately some strayed off the path and got in a bog. As they struggled forward to get out they sank further in. They were rescued however by other members. Their shoes were left behind. The incident caused great merriment, especially as some had to be fitted out with shoes.

Clarrie moved into the wooden bungalow recently vacated by his brother Tom and family who had left the district. He lived there for a number of years before moving into a new bungalow which he had built on the Keyham side of Scraptoft village. Clarrie was a keen gardener and grew his own vegetables on a plot of land at the rear of his new bungalow. Clarrie and Gertrude had a son, Ronald.

Keyham village was badly off for drinking water. Many of the cottages had to share with others who had outside pumps. Miss Healey at the village shop had to carry in buckets of water from the pump situated outside the cottage known as Horse Shoe Cottage. This was also used by the adjoining cottages. The cottages between the Dog and Gun and the school were supplied from the same source. At the top end of the village the pump in the stable yard of the Top Hall was used.

The new squire at the Top Hall decided to do something about this. A hand operated drilling derrick was erected on the spare piece of land opposite the stables of the Old Hall. Two men were engaged, one of them 'Old Sarg' lived in one of the charity cottages. The drilling was performed by the two men walking round and round in circles under the derrick, pressure was applied to the drill from a hand wheel screw arrangement above. The drill would be withdrawn from time to time and coves of clay examined. It was a laborious business which went on for several weeks. The boys in the village thought it great fun to watch, and teased the drillers asking them if they ever got giddy or how long it took to drill to Australia. The work was eventually abandoned as no water was found.

One September we had a heatwave, which lasted for two weeks. It was stiflingly hot, not only during the day but it continued during the night. It was so hot that four of us boys in the village decided that we would sleep out. We knew of a half built hayrick down in the fields near the Hungarton brook. There was a deep pool in the brook nearby and we planned to have a bathe in the early morning. We undressed and put on our pyjamas and climbed on the hayrick as it was getting dark. We settled down for the night but within a few minutes I think it was my brother who cried out 'I'm being bitten'. In a few minutes we were all being bitten. I think the hay was full of hungry insects or perhaps an ants' nest. As time went on it got worse, we were being bitten all over. We stood up and took off our pyjamas and shook them out. It was no good, we itched and scratched and sleep was impossible. It was dark and we could see nothing. We lay awake all night, and as it got light we packed to go home. The weather had changed and it had become cool. It was the end of the heat wave.

Squire Hincks' idea of farming did not work out as expected. There is no doubt that farming in the twenties and early thirties was difficult and unprofitable. He would without warning sack all his men when things went wrong. They would then be quickly replaced by others. This sort of thing must have happened three or four times to my knowledge during a period of ten to twelve years. This continuing change of staff was very upsetting to the village. The loss of cattle was high and it kept the knackerman – Texas Ross – busy from time to time. On one occasion some of the bullocks got in the Keyham Cemetery which is situated away from the village church along the Hungarton Road. They were feeding on the yew trees which soon proved fatal, as yew is deadly poisonous to animals. Before they were discovered several had died, their bodies lying on the graves.

The Misses Hincks always seemed to keep in the background irrespective of what was going on. The squire did not seem to be able to keep control over the farm and relied too much on his men. He had a certain amount of arable land, wheat, barley etc. We boys were always interested and around when threshing time came round. This always took place in the big stack-yard at Pear Tree Farm. In winter the engines usually got bogged down in the deep mud at the entrance. Visiting contractors usually carried out the work and took about a week. After a time the Squire decided to buy his own threshing tackle and thresh his own corn. He bought an old drum and steam engine. This engine was not designed or able to travel under its own power and had to be drawn by horses. You can imagine the difficulty in getting it lined up to the drum and the belt fixed. It had two large wooden wheels at the rear and a very high chimney with an ornamental serrated top. It looked very much like Stephenson's *Rocket*. It worked quite well however, in conjunction with a new elevator he bought. The elevator mechanism was driven by a horse walking round and round in circles. After a day's work the engine was covered over with a tarpaulin; at night we boys would sometimes creep up when the men had gone home and give the starting handle a nudge. The remaining steam would revolve the engine turning the fly wheel under the tarpaulin. We would turn the steam off and clear out of the way before we were discovered. The engine finally came to a sad end. The ejector pump failed and the boiler was short of water, but the operator failed to notice this and some of the tubes in the boiler started to leak. Repair was too expensive. It stayed in the stackyard for some years and finally ended up in the scrapyard.

One day an urgent request was received from one of the Directors of the Gimson Shoe Machinery Company. Apparently they were locked in battle with the British United in a High Court case in London. It was a question of the infringement of patent rights and if it could be proved that we made a certain casting on a certain date it might decide the result of the case. I was at work in the foundry at the time and was told to go up into the loft and wade through books and papers and advice notes: an accumulation of ten years. I spent most of the day in the loft when suddenly a message was received to say that a solution had been found. The two companies had decided to amalgamate and so ended the case. I believe from that time the Company has been known as The British United Shoe Machinery Company.

There was an occasion in the early twenties when we had a series of very severe frosts which lasted at least two weeks night and day. Suddenly one morning we had heavy rain which froze as it fell. The roads became too icy for any form of wheeled transport. I remember it being called a silver thaw. Certain important castings had been promised for delivery on that day and my father, sooner than let customers down, decided to carry them on his back and walk. Before setting out he cut two pieces out of an old motor inner tube. Slipping these tightly over his boots he started out much against my mother's appeals. He made it however and when he arrived, his customer in Vulcan Road, Gimsons, told him he was mad. I think this regular and unstinted attention to his customers won him the greatest respect. I heard them say 'If Bob Harrison can't do it, nobody can'.

During the early 1920s a General Strike took place. As we were not affiliated with any federation it did not affect us. Gimson Shoe Machinery Company asked my father if he could supply some iron castings; cams for a very important order for shoe machines scheduled for export on a certain boat. Their own iron foundry was on strike. They supplied him with some pig iron and the necessary patterns. The making of the moulds was no problem but the melting of iron in a natural draught coke fired pit furnace was another matter. The temperature required was 1500 C, for iron against the usual temperature for non-ferrous castings of 1200 C. By attending to the furnace himself and after great difficulties he finally succeeded. After many charges of coke it took 4 or 5 hours to melt 150 lbs charge to the required temperature. Sometimes it would not get hot enough and had to be poured down into a pig. A lot depended on the weather, strength of wind etc. The next problem was delivery, for their works were picketed by union officials. It was decided that the castings were to be put outside and then doused with plenty of water. This soon sent them rusty, the idea being that if discovered it could be said that they were old stock and had been made for some time. The rusty castings were placed in bags and thrown over the wall of the premises out of sight of the pickets. At last the strike was over and my father was released from this burden. It was some time after this that the shoe machinery side of Gimson's business was moved to a new factory built in Ulverscroft Road. This beautifully designed building with its matching cigar shaped chimney is I believe now occupied by Bostik Ltd.

After the Seal family had moved from the Nether Hall the Harris family were next to live there. They were Quakers and proved to be very nice people. They took a keen interest in the village. Mr Alec Harris and Mrs Rebecca Harris had one son Tom, who went to Cambridge, and three daughters, Ruth, Rebecca and Anna. Mr Harris was a tall professor type and an inventor. He soon had a well-equipped work shop in the Hall yard. Nether Hall had its own electric supply with storage accumulators which provided him with the necessary power. He invented a bed with the trade name of 'Ne'er sag'. This apparently infringed a patent of a bed called the 'Sleepezee'; a High Court case was held in London and unfortunately Mr Harrris lost the case. He also operated in Leicester a small business called The Gripper Company. They made all types of tongues, fire tongs, sugar tongs etc. They were made of brass and a special design. The castings were made in the foundry. Mr Harris was an eccentric type and sometimes absent-minded. He would occasionally walk into the foundry, hesitate, and then walk out.

In the garden at the Nether Hall, beyond the lawn, was a shrubbery of laurel bushes. These were old and well-established. He wanted them removed with explosive. A charge was laid among the roots and a long fuse was ignited. After a terrific explosion we in the yard at The White House were showered in earth and small stones. This happened several times until my father complained asking him if he did not realise the danger. Alec finally got rid of the trees and dug out the roots and peace was restored.

On another occasion he needed to go to the village of Scraptoft. His daughter Ruth was driving into town and he decided to let her tow him on a bicycle as far as Scraptoft, no doubt his idea was to cycle back. Unfortunately while going down Keyham Hill the tow rope got caught round the front wheel, and he came off and was badly cut and bruised and grazed on his face. He had to attend hospital and it was some weeks before he recovered.

The Harris family had a big old fashioned car which was quite old and was always breaking down. It was advertised for sale several times but without result. Mrs Harris put a very nicely worded advertisement in the Leicester Mercury. The last sentence read 'not suitable for anyone living on a hill'. The ad caused much amusement and next day my father was asked by several of his customers who was the person living at Keyham wanting to sell a car which wouldn't climb hills. The car remained unsold. Tom was studying Geology at Cambridge and was chosen to accompany a two-year trip to the Antarctic and Polar regions. His particular part was the study of fossils and marine life. On his return he gave a very interesting lecture in the school room on his travels and experiences, including his encounter with a polar bear.

The Harris family were very interested in researching the history of Keyham. Mr Harris gave a very interesting lecture. The family were also interested in amateur dramatics and they put on a show with some of their friends which was called 'The Elixir of Life'. Mr Harris took the principal part of The Professor. The school room was full and the show was much enjoyed.

Tom Harris was on holiday from Cambridge and one morning we were all sitting round the table at The White House having breakfast. Suddenly the door was opened and Tom's face appeared with one foot in the door. He said in his best Cambridge voice 'I've just come round from the Nether'. My father looked up and said 'You can bugger off back to The

Decorative hearth stand, moulded and cast by the author.

Door knocker cast by the author.

Nether'. Tom disappeared but later on came round and apologised, although we never learnt what his earlier visit was about.

During 1927 there were quite a few young people in the village and not much in the way of entertainment. This was most noticeable during the long winter months. There was no village hall, and although the school was always available for hire this did not fit in with what was required for various reasons. Mr Harris at The Nether Hall suggested getting together and forming an evening institution. The Misses Hincks were approached and approved the idea. They offered free a sizeable room over one of the outbuildings at the Top Hall. It had a fireplace and an electric light from their private supply. The room needed decorating but with plenty of willing hands a committee was formed and the room was soon made shipshape. The Misses Hincks made no charge for the facilities and supplied a loudspeaker which was wired to their radio receiver. This was switched on for the church service on Sunday nights at 8pm. A small charge was made for membership for covering the running expenses of the coal fire etc. There was a good gathering of members both male and female. It was open for two nights a week plus Sunday night. This was during the winter months. Games were supplied, dominoes, draughts, playing cards etc. Some time later, a half-sized second-hand billiard table was acquired, which proved very popular. We had some very enjoyable evenings but sad to say late one night the room caught fire and was badly damaged. It was thought that the beam in the chimney had caught alight. This brought our social activities to an end.

My mother's health had always been good as had the rest of the family. My father in particular never seemed to ail, he never had colds and was always fit and well. My mother had recently complained of feeling unwell with pains and our local doctor, Doctor Ellison of Syston was called and he suggested she should have a thorough examination. My father arranged this at the Faire Hospital, Causeway Lane, Leicester. This was situated at the rear of the maternity hospital where my youngest sister Marjorie was born. The examination report was that an operation was necessary. A Mr Cumberledge was engaged, a very well known physician. My mother was admitted and the operation performed and all seemed well. My mother was soon home and after a few weeks' convalescence was able to get about and resume her normal duties.

We were very glad to have her back as we had to look after ourselves during her absence. It had been a very worrying time. My sisters looked after the house and cooked the meals. My father made sure we had enough to eat and cooked the Sunday lunch. After several months when we thought my mother had made a complete recovery she was again taken ill. This proved serious and another operation was necessary. My mother again recovered and after some weeks came home. After this she suffered a lot of serious pain. My brother or I would race down to Beeby on our cycles to the nearest phone at the

Manor House, where the lady of the house would phone for Doctor Ellison at Syston. He was very good and always came promptly. He was able to relieve her of the pain with injections. In those days there were no pain relieving tablets as today. My eldest sister was marvellous, attending my mother and performing the duties which really required a trained nurse.

My father suggested to Doctor Ellison that one of his bungalows up at Hillcrest was vacant; the doctor agreed a complete change of environment was what she needed. We decided we would all move up there to be with her. We transferred beds and necessary furniture for a short stay. That year, 1925, we had a beautiful summer. My mother had a bed near the open double doors. As her illness became worse a trained nurse was engaged to look after her. We children were told by my father that our mother would not get better as her illness was cancer. This news caused us all great distress. My mother passed away on June 21st 1925. We were a very close knit family, our mother and father meant everything to us. I was seventeen at the time, my youngest sister Marjorie was four. Our stay at the bungalow had been for about six months, after which we returned to The White House.

The death of my mother caused great concern to my father and of course the rest of us. He had his business to look after and at the same time a family of six children. We were all fairly well domesticated: my mother had seen to that. Both my brother and I were working in the foundry at the time. My father immediately advertised locally for a housekeeper. It soon became apparent it would be difficult to find a person willing and able to fill the position. However, he had replies which resulted in interviews and trial engagements. None proved suitable for various reasons. It was a very worrying time. A further advertisement was tried further afield. This proved more successful. A lady replied who lived at Ilford in Essex. She held a responsible position in a children's home. An interview was arranged and a visit to Keyham. Her name was Mrs Alice Dorrell, a widow. The interview was favourable and after a further visit she was offered the position as housekeeper which she decided to accept.

She commenced her duties after giving notice to her present employers. Mrs Dorrell had a daughter Mildred, aged 14, who was living with her aged grandparents at Grays in Essex. Some months after that my father and Mrs Dorrell considered marriage. Before this took place he paid a visit to my mother's home at Woodford to explain the situation. He took with him my youngest sister Marjorie, who was aged five at the time. It was decided that if the marriage took place, Mildred would become one of the family.

My father was married at St Nicholas Church, Holy Bones, Leicester in the presence of Tom Spiers, an old friend, and my Aunt Louie. The idea of a stepmother did not really appeal to us as there could never be anyone to replace our mother. We decided we would call our stepmother auntie. As we all settled down this worked out quite well. From now on, however, I will refer to her as Alice.

Due to my mother's illness, and after her death, my father had to find someone to take over the clerical side of the business. A Mr Moores, who occupied a responsible position in the offices of Messrs Gimson and Co., came to his rescue. He agreed to take over the whole of the responsibility of the book keeping, invoicing and any correspondence that was necessary. This he carried out entirely in his own spare time.

He would meet my father at Causeway Lane every Wednesday during his lunch break and again on Saturday morning, occasionally coming over to Keyham on his motor bike during weekends. Mr Moores carried out these duties from 1926 until extra commitments at Gimsons gave him no time to attend to our clerical work. Before this happened he decided, or he suggested, that I should take over these duties. He taught me double entry book keeping, purchasing and sales ledger and how to balance the cash book, all in a few weeks. Fortunately he was always available in the evenings and at weekends to put me right. I carried on this extra work for about nine months in my spare time after my work in the foundry and at weekends.

I never expected that the answer to my problem might be overcome by a member of the family. It was decided that my youngest sister, Marjorie, would take a three-month business training course at the Leicester College. I continued for a further three months until she was able to take over this side of the business. A second-hand Underwood typewriter was purchased for £15. This was a great step forward. In the past all correspondence, invoices etc. were hand written.

It was agreed that the time had come to create some office accommodation. I, like my mother, used a room in The White House for this part of the business. A small room of part of the rear premises at Causeway Lane was fitted out and made comfortable, heated with an electric fire and fitted with a telephone. Artificial lighting was necessary during the day. Marjorie was ready to relieve me of the clerical side of the business and she managed this very well, working from 9am to 5pm. This enabled me to concentrate on other necessary work.

As the end of the twenties approached trade was dwindling. Orders were difficult to obtain. The recession was settling in. My father relied on the local engineers for his orders for castings. They were in great difficulties themselves and he was obliged to dismiss his eight employees. I was told to keep the foundry at Causeway Lane open. My brother Robert did the same at Keyham. My father called on all his customers every day to see if anything might be wanted. I would be aged 20 at the time and my brother 18. We had been well-trained by my father and encouraged to work hard since leaving school. At the age of 14 we had been working 48 hours per week.

Things got worse and then the Midland Bank foreclosed on the mortgage and demanded immediate repayment of £1,600 my father had

Pouring aluminium into a mould at the Gough Road works.

'The Game Keeper' a door stop moulded and cast by the author.

borrowed to buy Causeway Lane. The Bank had asked for his balance sheet as they did every year and they did not like what they saw. The local manager of the small branch of the Midland Bank had his instructions from London and despite my father's pleading to give him a chance he was refused.

It looked like the end after all the hard work during and since the war. He decided to put our home up for sale. An estate agent Messrs Warner Shepherd and Wade was engaged. A brochure was printed and this advertised the house to be sold by auction at the Bell Hotel, Humberstone Gate, Leicester. When the time came for the sale no one had been to look round the house; this did not bode well. Mr Tom Spiers, a well known Leicester business man who owned an iron foundry and was a friend of my father, accompanied him to the sale. (Tom used to swear a lot). He said 'I'll see the buggers don't get your house'. As the sale commenced there was hardly anyone in the room except the estate agents. Not a single bid was recorded; this gives some idea of the state of the recession at the time.

My father was back to square one. A week or two later some one suggested he approach a well-known firm of solicitors in New Street, Leicester. He was received with great courtesy by the head of the firm. The outcome was that they were willing to lend him the £1,600 on the basis of a 5% interest charge. It was trust money. He was told he could have this for as long as he liked at the fixed rate of 5% providing the interest was paid regularly. He was saved. (The loan was repaid in 1939, with some of the proceeds from the compulsory sale of Causeway Lane to Leicester Corporation.) With his cheque book in his hand he paid a visit to Midland Bank repaying the loan and closing his account and telling them in no uncertain manner what he thought of them. He then approached Barclays Bank at Gallowtree Gate, asking if they were willing for him to open an account. This was granted. The Bank Manager commented that 'as banks we do not talk about one another but we do think you have had a raw deal'. Thus it was Barclays who from then on to the present day were the firm's bankers.

During the late twenties electricity came to Keyham, provided by the Leicester and Warwickshire Power Supply Company. The foundry was one of the first to be connected. We were now able to have a single phased power supply. This was used to work a new forced draught coke-fired furnace with a capacity of 80 lbs. This was a great improvement, as up to eight casts a day could be obtained. The old slow natural draught furnaces were only used when large melts were required. My brother Robert took charge of the melting with the new furnace.

It had for a time become apparent that to continue the foundry at Keyham would be a mistake. At the rear of the Causeway Lane foundry was an old, fairly spacious, building. The brickwork was removed to form a doorway entrance into the new part.

Electricity and a concrete floor were installed. There were skylights in the roof. Up in the small loft I arranged for oil tanks to be fixed as it was decided to melt the metal using oil. This was becoming general practice in non-ferrous foundries. Two new bale-out oil fired furnaces were installed, fed by gravity from the oil tanks above. We had been making aluminium alloy castings for several years at Keyham and it now seemed the time to expand this side of the business.

In 1931 both my brother Robert and myself, being twenty one years of age, were eligible to be sworn in and become members of The Freemen of Leicester. This ceremony is carried out by the Lord Mayor in the Lord Mayor's Chamber at the Town Hall. It is usual, when possible, for the father to be present and to introduce his sons. I remember my father saying: 'I have brought my sons to be enrolled as Freemen and I have their birth certificates', and placing them on the table in front of the Lord Mayor. No words were spoken by the Lord Mayor and in fact he never even looked up during the ceremony. We signed our names on the necessary forms and took our leave. It was all over in three minutes. The Lord Mayor during that year was Alderman Carver. What a difference when I took my own son, David, to be enrolled as a Freeman. We were made welcome and shook hands all round. The Lord Mayor asked for details of the work he was doing. He had a photographer present who took a photograph of David holding a Bible whilst taking the oath of the Freemen. During 1994 my sons Robert and Brian were also enrolled as Freemen.

Robert Harrison, joint Managing Director of R.C. Harrison & Son, being enrolled as a Freeman.

Chapter Six

Keyham and Gough Road

I advertised for young men to be taught moulding and the foundry trade in general; three were taken on. I am pleased to say that under my guidance and tuition these young men became expert craftsmen. They stayed with us for more than 25 years; one completed 40 years. I think this expansion proved a turning point in our business. The expansion during 1936 in the existing buildings at the rear of the brass shop was only allowed on a temporary basis by the City Corporation because the buildings were already there. It had been made quite clear to my father that the whole premises were likely to be compulsorily purchased as it was a slum clearance area but they could not say when this was likely to take place. My brother and I carried on until about 1938. I was managing the Leicester site and my brother Robert at Keyham.

The country was at this time in a state of re-arming. Germany was already armed to the hilt. We in this country were totally unprepared. The Ministry of Supply was urging all foundries and engineers to concentrate on the production of machine tools which were in very short supply. Leicester was well equipped with Machine Tool manufacturers. They were likely to keep us busy for some time. My father, realising that we would have to move, started looking out for suitable premises or land to build on.

This was very difficult as the Corporation was strongly against foundries in towns especially near built up areas. After a time my father took a chance and bought a plot of land in Gough Road, Leicester. The whole of this area was allotments and completely undeveloped with no roads. It was soon after this that the Corporation filed a compulsory purchase order on the Causeway Lane site. My brother and I had already made up our minds that we would close the foundry at Keyham when the time came to move. After the purchase of the land no further finance was available for progress. Everything depended on the council's valuation of the Causeway Lane site property. My father tried to engage Tarratts the well known Leicester Estate Agents to act for him on the valuation but the Corporation had already engaged them to represent their interests. My father decided to engage Sir Stanhope Rollestone, a well known estate agent, to represent him. Then the battle commenced. Finally the sum of

£4600 was agreed. Now we could go ahead with further plans. My father engaged an architect to prepare plans to build in Gough Road. The plans were turned down by the planning department for environmental reasons. After further appeals the building department relented and the plans were passed. A building contractor Messrs Sharp and Co., of Leicester were engaged and the building commenced. It was built for the sum of £5000, mainly with the proceeds of the sale of Causeway Lane. A penalty clause of £8 per week was placed on the builder if it was not finished on time. It was a fine-looking building with the office block at the front with a pantile roof. On its completion during 1939 my father must have been a very proud man. His customers were pleased and remarked 'Bob's on a winner this time'.

We moved into the new premises just before the Second World War. Much remained to be done. The garden soil inside had to be removed and in its place a hundred tons of iron foundry black sand put down and rolled firm to make a floor. Later on after a number of years the sand was removed and a concrete floor was laid. We had no overhead crane, this was added later. A three-ton hand-operated crane covered one of the bays. The site my father chose for the new foundry was at the end of the adopted part of Gough Road; thus we had to get to the site over unmade roads, very uneven and full of potholes. However, we had to put up with this until we could afford to have the road made up. Eventually a concrete road was built. Messrs Brown and Shaw, building contractors, also decided to buy land and build a factory opposite the foundry. They agreed

Employees at the Gough Rd foundry in 1940, in this photograph are George Kirby, Jack Platt, Cliff Holmes, Johny Williams, and Charlie Latham.

to pay their share for the building of the road and were awarded the contract. This gave us both good access to our works. (Messrs Brown and Shaw were the firm that built the six agricultural cottages at Keyham facing Kings Lane and Ingarsby Road).

The time had now arrived for my father to take things easier. He was able to leave the running of the business to my brother and I, but remained well in the picture. We were given a completely free hand. Our policy was one of ploughing back all the profits into the company and keeping our plant up to date. Most of our customers were local and we became the principal supplier of non-ferrous castings in this area.

We were officially approved by the Aeronautical Inspection Directorate (AID) and the Admiralty, and we were regularly visited by their inspectors. Many interesting castings were made during the War. We often worked late at night and over the weekend. There was a great shortage of non-ferrous metal, especially aluminium alloys: every pound had to be accounted for and was only allowed to be used by authorisation of the Ministry of Supply and only then for the War effort.

Probably the most arduous task in a non-ferrous foundry is the furnaceman. I am referring to the days when natural and forced draught coke fired furnaces were in general use. This would be around the early '30s and before.

Our furnaceman, Jack Muggleton, lived at Hungarton and would arrive on his cycle at Gough Road at 7.30am. It was in the afternoon when things got really busy and the moulders were crying out for molten metal. I went into the furnace department on a very hot summer's day. Jack was sweating and swearing. Three furnaces were blazing away, the flames coming out from the top and what with the noise of the motor fans, Jack came over to me and he said 'Govner, there must be better bloody jobs in hell than this'. Jack stayed with us as furnaceman for many years.

Over the next few years we changed our method of melting to oil and gas. This greatly improved working conditions and many years later we changed to electricity, known as induction melting.

Jack was always fond of horses and accepted an offer of a job at Baggrave Hall with Sir George and Lady Earle. He was to be personal groom to Lady Earle. She was a side saddle rider. He told me that one day he was holding her horse ready for her to mount. He noticed she was limping a little. 'Had a fall, my lady?', he asked. 'Yes, it's my bloody arse', she replied. Jack stayed with the Earles until they left Baggrave Hall.

One of the hazards encountered at the Gough Road foundry was a brook, known as Willow Brook. It flowed through Humberstone Park and past the rear of the foundry, and was wild and neglected. Melting snow and heavy rain would raise the brook to within a foot of the foundry floor. Leicester Corporation, whose responsibility it was, would sometimes attempt to clean it out. Over the years it got worse until one Saturday, after prolonged and heavy rain it flowed into the foundry in spite of the doors being sandbagged. I telephoned the Town Hall who quickly sent down some of the Councillors including the Town Clerk. They arrived with their wellington boots. The water had run into the furnace pits and other underground works. They were very alarmed when they saw what had happened. It was soon decided that the length of the Brook would be bricked on both sides. The water had to be diverted in concrete pipes; it proved a big and costly job. When it was half-finished the contractors went bankrupt, which meant further delay whilst another firm was appointed. When completed it was an excellent job forming a seven foot wide channel eight feet deep, all in high class brick. A smaller channel was formed at the centre bottom. This normally carried all the water under normal conditions.

One of the greatest difficulties for foundries during the war was the lack of labourers. This meant some of the skilled men staying on after their day's work, joining with my brother and I in knocking out the moulds and mixing the sand ready for an early start the next morning.

We received orders from Powerjets of Whetstone. This was during the development of the jet engine by Sir Frank Whittle. It was during October 1941 that the Government decided to build a new factory for Powerjets at Whetstone. This was to further the development of the jet engine. We

Frank Whittle and Mr Rout (pattern shop manager) at Power Jets at Whetstone, with the scale model of the jet engine made by R. C. Harrison and Sons Ltd. The engine is now in the Science Museum in London.

became very much involved and were asked to supply aluminium alloy castings for the project. These consisted of the main compressor casings and other parts and were cast at Gough Road. My brother, Robert, was closely associated with this. He made frequent visits to their pattern shop at Whetstone to arrange with their head pattern makers how the patterns were to be made to our moulding requirements. This association continued throughout the war with Powerjets until the manufacture of jet engines was taken over by the Rolls Royce Company at Derby. A complete set of castings for a scale model of the W2/700 engine was made at Gough Road. This is now on exhibition in the Science Museum in London.

During 1987 Sir Frank Whittle was invited back to Lutterworth where his early experiments commenced. This was for the unveiling of a bronze bust in his honour.

The Francis family came to live at Keyham sharing accommodation with the family living at Mayfield Farm by the name of Carter. There was Mr and Mrs Francis and their two sons, Leslie and Douglas and one daughter, Irene. Mr Francis had been head gardener for the Burnabys at Baggrave Hall before coming to Keyham.

Leslie and I became great friends. We had much in common – amateur radio, motor cycles etc. He was a regular visitor to the foundry yard

The bust of Sir Frank Whittle by Kenneth Ford, situated in Church Street Gardens, Lutterworth.

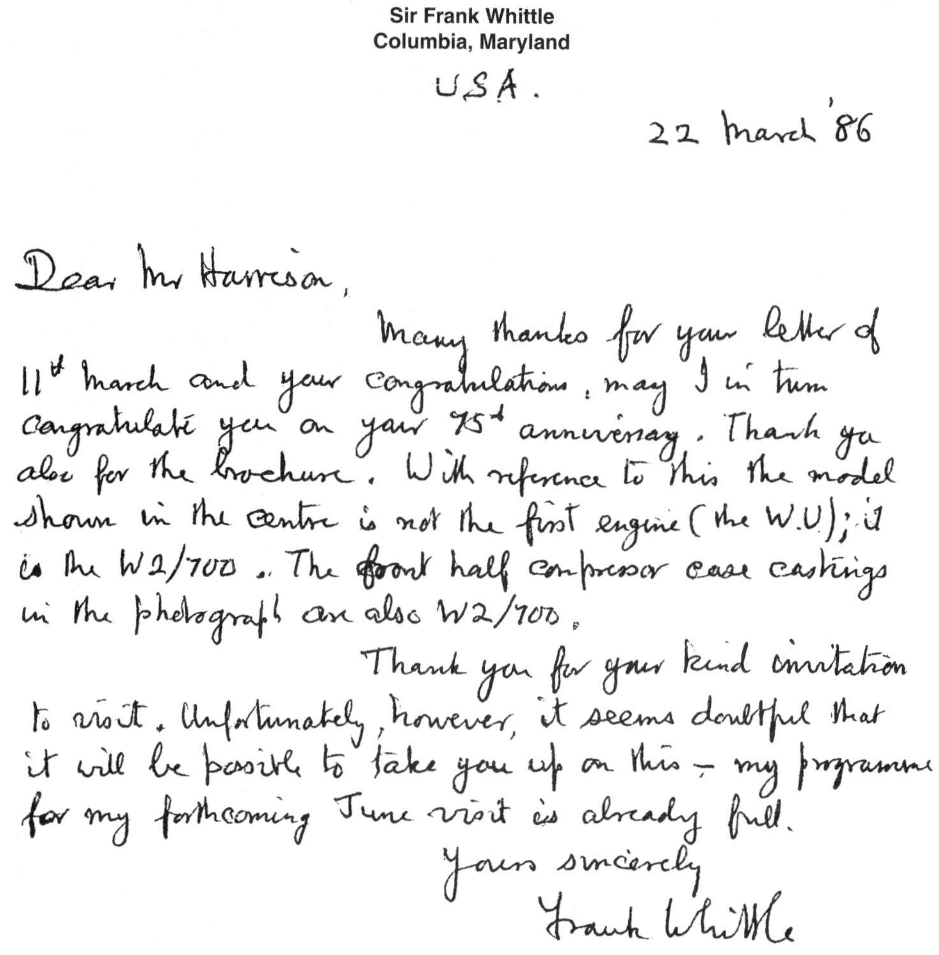

Sir Frank Whittle
Columbia, Maryland

USA.

22 March '86

Dear Mr Harrison,

Many thanks for your letter of 11th March and your congratulations; may I in turn congratulate you on your 75th anniversary. Thank you also for the brochure. With reference to this the model shown in the centre is not the first engine (the W.U); it is the W2/700. The front half compressor case castings in the photograph are also W2/700.

Thank you for your kind invitation to visit. Unfortunately, however, it seems doubtful that it will be possible to take you up on this — my programme for my forthcoming June visit is already full.

Yours sincerely

Frank Whittle

Letter from Frank Whittle to Mr Harrison.

among the old cars. His father was a highly skilled gardener especially in the greenhouse. He obtained a job at a large house in Stoneygate owned by a Mr Jones. Sometimes when he arrived for work on his cycle at 8am he would find Mr Jones fast asleep drunk on the steps. His wife had apparently locked him out.

Leslie found employment at The Cottage where lived a Mr and Mrs Adams of Adams Bros. and Shardlow, Printers. Leslie was taught to drive and act as chauffeur to Mrs Adams. He also helped out in the garden. They supplied him with a new bull-nosed Morris 2 seater. It was Leslie who coined the phrase 'bed tick' for the nickname for the Keyham bus.

The Francis family stayed in the village for about two years and then they moved on to Banstead in Surrey where Mr Francis obtained a job as

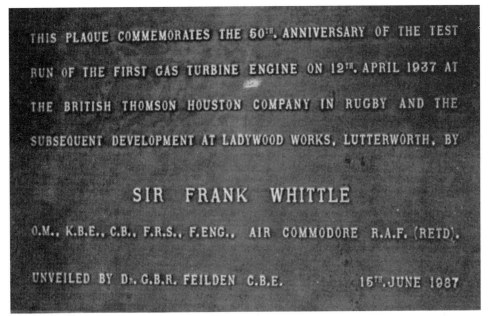

THIS PLAQUE COMMEMORATES THE 50TH. ANNIVERSARY OF THE TEST

RUN OF THE FIRST GAS TURBINE ENGINE ON 12TH. APRIL 1937 AT

THE BRITISH THOMSON HOUSTON COMPANY IN RUGBY AND THE

SUBSEQUENT DEVELOPMENT AT LADYWOOD WORKS, LUTTERWORTH, BY

SIR FRANK WHITTLE

O.M., K.B.E., C.B., F.R.S., F.ENG., AIR COMMODORE R.A.F. (RETD).

UNVEILED BY D. G.B.R. FEILDEN C.B.E.   15TH.JUNE 1987

Plaque commemorating the 50th anniversary of the test run of the first Gas Turbine engine in 1937. Made and donated by R.C. Harrison & Sons Ltd.

head gardener for the Garton family of H.P. Sauce fame. This was a beautiful estate with a very large house with its own ballroom. My brother and I were invited to stay for a week's holiday with them. This was during August. We travelled up to London by train where we met Mrs Francis who travelled with us and showed us the way to their house, the gardener's cottage at Banstead. The Garton family were on holiday at the time. We had the run of the garden and grounds and had a very enjoyable time.

Some months after our return we learned that Leslie had acquired a BSA motorcycle. They paid us a visit on this, Douglas riding pillion. My brother and I wanted to follow suit. I saw an advertisement for a second-hand two stroke two speed Campion with a Villiers engine that was belt driven. It was owned by a Doctor at Newtown Linford. The asking price was £27 but when I explained that I was new to motor cycling and knew very little about them the Doctor kindly tied a label on all the various controls stating their use. My father was not at all keen on us having motor cycles but a deal was arranged and my father agreed to collect it on the back of the lorry. I accompanied him and we arrived home with the labels fluttering in the breeze. I soon learned to ride it but it was not until some time later that I decided that it was not such a good buy. I will explain why later on.

My brother heard of a second-hand AJS motor cycle, 2¾ h.p., which often appeared in the village. He pursuaded the owner to part with it and sell it to him, which he finally did for £15. This was a very good buy. Three speed all chain drive and it lasted him for some years.

Both my brother and I were now mobile and this enabled us to meet our friends, the Francis boys, Leslie and Douglas half way. Sometimes this would be at Northampton or Bedford where we would have a picnic before returning home.

It was on one of these trips on a Sunday to Bedford that we passed the airship sheds at Cardington which housed the airship R101. There were a lot of people milling around the hangar and we learned later that they were waiting for news as the airship had crashed in France on its maiden voyage.

It was during a run in heavy rain, the road full of puddles, that I got left behind after some miles. The others found I was missing and waited for me. I caught up with them eventually travelling at about 15 mph. The rubber belt on my machine had got wet and was slipping. It would not grip. When I got home I tried to tighten the belt applying resin but it was no good. I had acquired a dry weather bike. I was made fun of after this and Leslie would say when the roads were wet we will give you a half hour start. There was nothing unusual about belt driven motor bikes in those days before the chain drive came into general use. All suffered with belt slip when the roads were wet.

Keyham 'bikers' left to right: Douglas Francis, Robert Harrison, Clarrie Timson and the author. The photograph taken by Leslie Francis *c*. 1930.

I decided that I could not put up with this and I wanted to acquire something better. Looking through the adverts in the local paper I saw on offer a BSA 493 cc overhead valve model. I made an appointment to view. It was little more than a year old and had cost £65 when new. It was a beautiful bike, with the new style saddle tank. The engine was inclined forward and had a swept back exhaust system. I went back home to see if I could raise the £35 asking price. This I managed to do after I sold the Campion for £15.

My brother, seeing my new mount, decided to have a change and soon acquired a very nice second-hand Ariel 500 cc overhead valve model. We were both now well equipped to go anywhere.

We went on holiday with our friends the Francises to the Isle of Wight. The roads were quite a delight to travel on in those days with very little traffic. The smooth tarmacadam surface could be quite treacherous when it rained and we had the greasy tram lines to contend with in the towns. I once had a spill caused by these but fortunately I was not seriously hurt.

My father was concerned if my brother and I were late home at night and was known to get out the lorry to look for us.

Having two acres of land including the paddock to play on, my brother and I were always thinking of some plan of entertainment. The garden, as a result of the foundry, became derelict and we were allowed to do more or less what we liked.

With some of the youths in the village we formed a race track for push bikes. This consisted of a circle about 50 feet in diameter covered in loose soil. We obtained some old bikes from the village that had seen better days, and spent some time making them with new tyres fit to ride, etc. They were then stripped of brakes and mudguards and anything unnecessary. The front wheel and forks were turned back to front. This shortened the wheel base and made cornering easier. We had great fun racing one another – broadsiding around the corners and skidding about. When we had visitors to come to see us, uncles, aunts, cousins, friends etc. we would give them a demonstration. They were real townies and not used to visiting the country very often. I think they thought we were mad, and they could not stop laughing especially when one of us went over the handlebars. As we got more skilled and daring the bikes became the worse for wear. Wheels would buckle and frames became distorted. My brother had an idea. He took his bike into the foundry, took off the saddle and then poured molten aluminium into the frame. This strengthened the frame but made it rather heavy. The result was he came last in the race. There were no strong mountain bikes in those days.

One year we took the bikes to a garden fete at Houghton on the Hill. A cycle race was one of the attractions on the programme and three of us decided to enter with our old bikes. All of the other competitors were on ordinary bikes and were not very pleased when they saw what we had – no brakes etc. I think they thought we might run into them and they tried to get us barred from entering. The officials, however, let us compete. We all joined up in a row and off we went. Our track bikes being light and low-geared shot to the front well ahead of the others. We led for about three laps cheered on by the crowd and then a chap with a three speed gear model caught up with us and passed us on the last lap to win the race.

The heavy falls of snow which were experienced most winters in Keyham were always welcomed by the young people in the village. We made our own sledges using sheet aluminium for the bottom of the sledge. Unlike the commercial type with narrow runners which were only suitable for hard packed frozen snow, ours were very fast, even on newly fallen snow. They were big enough for three or four. A rope about ten feet long was attached to the sledge. This was to recover it out of the brook. The cricket field was the favourite run. We had to roll off the sledge, staying on as long as we dared, and letting the sledge go over the bank and into the brook. Sometimes two or three of the young men from the foundry would borrow the sledge in their dinner hour accompanied by Robert. On one occasion they misjudged their speed, staying on too long and landing in the brook. They were wet through. Alice had to find them some dry clothes before they could resume work.

It was around 1930 that we heard officially that Keyham was at last to have a village hall. Hungarton had already built theirs which was opened during 1928. I understand most of the money for the building came from the Carnegie Trust. Keyham had however subscribed towards it by raising money by holding various social functions over the years. The opening ceremony was performed by Mrs Cheales, who came over with her husband from Lincolnshire to perform it. This was by the cutting of a ribbon which was stretched across the doorway. This was followed by a high tea for everyone who attended.

Now we could have whist drives, concerts, and dances. There would be no more carrying out the heavy school desks into the school playground when we wanted a dance. It really was a great asset – fully centrally heated by a hot water radiator system from an outside coke-fired boiler. We still had to find money, however, to furnish it. Wooden chairs and small card tables were obtained. On big occasions, Hungarton would lend us their tables and chairs. It was my job, having a lorry, to collect and return them, which I did for a number of years until we were able to afford our own furniture. A second-hand piano was purchased which gave good service for many years. This, together with a violin and a saxophone, were all that was needed. Dances were held regularly in several of the villages – Barsby, Hungarton, Tilton and Houghton on the Hill.

The dances at Tilton were very popular, being held on a Friday night. They extended until 2am. We had motor cycles by those days, so transport was no difficulty.

I remember my brother Robert got out one of the old veteran cars. He got it running in the yard and we decided to attend a dance at Houghton on the Hill. There was usually a policeman on duty at dances at Houghton and therefore as the car was not licensed or taxed we had to be careful. The car ran beautifully, but we decided not to take it up into the village but to hide it behind a hedge in a field a few hundred yards from the village. After the dance we asked some of our girl dancing partners who had walked from Hungarton if they would like a ride home. They jumped at the chance. When we got outside they said 'Where's the car?' When we explained we had hidden it behind a hedge in a field down the road, they hesitated and looked at one another not quite sure whether to accept our offer. However, we managed to convince them they had nothing to fear and would be all right. They accompanied us to the car amid much laughter. Robert opened the gate and drove out the veteran car. This caused further consternation. Was it safe? However, we all crammed in and arrived back safely.

I must relate a second experience I had with a church bier. This was one which belonged to Keyham Village Church and had been used from time to time before and since the turn of the century until the early 1930s, Keyham cemetery being about a quarter of a mile from the village.

At a meeting of the Parochial Church Council it was decided that it was unlikely to be required in the future and I, being at that time one of the church wardens, was asked to try and dispose of it. I decided to advertise it in the Leicester Mercury using my address and telephone number. I was surprised to receive a call the first night the advertisement appeared. It was from a young lady in her early twenties who said she was very interested and would like to buy it. I told her it was at Keyham and suggested she ought to come over and have a look at it. But no, she said 'If you can deliver it to me at my address at Kedleston Road, between 12 and 1 o'clock while I am at home from work, I will buy it'. I told her the price – I think it was about £60. She seemed satisfied with this. With our lorry and driver we loaded it up and set off. She was waiting at the front gate. I could see it would not go through the gate. She said 'If you take it around the back through the garden the gate is wider'. We found our way to the rear of the house up a narrow service road which led to the rear of the houses. It was too narrow to take any vehicle. The bier was therefore unloaded and we made our way pushing it up the service road. She was waiting for us at the gate. This also was too narrow, but by tipping it on one side we managed to get it through. It was a long garden up to the back door. I was looking for a shed or some sort of cover to put it in but she wanted it in the house. Again by tipping it on its side we had a great struggle to get it in. Then we had a surprise. She said, 'I want it in my bedroom, will you get it upstairs'. The driver looked at me and whispered 'we've got a right one here'. I said 'Aren't you going to clean it up – the wheels are all rusty – you can't take it upstairs like that'. She said she knew someone down the road who might clean it up for her. She added 'Some people think it odd that I collect things like this. Be sure and let me know if you get anything else similar'. Out came her cheque book – the deal was soon settled and away we came.

Keyham village hall has always had very special memories for me because it was here when I was running regular fortnightly dances that I met Muriel, my future wife. She lived in Leicester and was invited to come and stay the night with her friend Mary Lester at one of the bungalows at Hill Crest. The dances were usually held on Saturday nights and proved very popular, attracting up to seventy or eighty dancers. Entrance was 1/6d and dancing was from 8pm to 11.45. Midland Red were running a bus service at this time. The last bus left for Leicester at 11.45pm.

There were three in the band who charged £1.10s.0d. for their services (today's price £1.50). Refreshments were supplied, and charged extra – tea, coffee, sandwiches and cakes. On alternate Saturdays a whist drive was held.

Special dances were held near Christmas when the room would be decorated. On New Year's Eve a fancy dress dance would be held to raise money in aid of the cricket club. These entertainments went on until 1939 and the war then put a stop to them when the Home Guard was formed. They had a claim for its use until the end of the war.

Squire Hincks was well known in agricultural circles and was on various committees. He was chosen to accompany a party of farmers to visit the Argentine, representing Leicestershire farmers and accompanied by his daughter Emily. This choice was not popular with the local farmers in view of the way his own farm was run.

One day during the early 1930s, he asked me up to the Hall. I was invited into his study. Miss Emily was with him. Apparently he was interested in buying some shares and asked for my advice. I was in no position to advise on shares, having never owned one in my life but in this particular case the firm was connected with foundries and he wanted my advice. I told him what I thought and understand that afterwards my advice proved profitable. I was offered a glass of vintage port. I had been warned about this vintage port and being a bit wary I declined a second glass.

He explained to me that they came to farm at Keyham during 1919 with big ideas but things had proved very disappointing. After many years of difficult farming conditions, it was noticeable that he was taking less interest in farming; he decided to let the tenancy of the four farms in the village. As time went on, he started indulging in horse racing. He acquired several racehorses and started breeding using the stables adjoining the Top Hall. He engaged a head groom, a Mr Sleath, who occupied a corner cottage at the top of the village, near to the stables. Some of the horses eventually were put out to trainers and were entered for races, but I cannot recall any great success. He did win a race or two and sometimes came second on a horse called Hiperian. Sometimes the horses would be exercised out in his own fields as part of their training, ridden by Sleath and a stable boy.

Keyham had its own blacksmith's shop which was well equipped mainly for the shoeing of horses. It was owned by the Squire and let to various blacksmiths over the years. One of the tenants, named Payne, a brother and sister working together, ran the business for a number of years. The sister was very strong and over six feet tall and a muscular woman. She dressed like a man and had a voice like a man. I remember one day she came down to the foundry to deliver a tool made for us. In the yard a labourer was breaking pig iron. This was during the time my father was casting iron. Pig iron, in those days, came in lengths of about 4 feet by 4 ins by 3 ins thick. A 14 lb sledge-hammer was used. The labourer wasn't making much progress. The lady took the hammer, swinging it high over her head and each time the hammer came down the pig iron was broken, sometimes in two or more places. Her strength was amazing. In about ten minutes she had broken enough pig iron to last for the week. At the forge she was a wonderful striker.

Keyham had its own slaughterhouse and I was told that this was in use during the turn of the century. It was a brick building, adjacent to a walled grassed area where the cattle were held. This lead into the slaughterhouse through a narrow passage with a door at each end. A pole-axe was used in those days for killing. I can remember this hanging on one of the walls. Many hooks were fastened on the beams across the roof on which to hang the carcasses. It occupied a site on the opposite side of the road in front of West End Farm. The slaughterhouse was used by the Fielding family – butchers of Houghton on the Hill. Mr and Mrs Fielding used to deliver the meat once a week to Keyham.

I remember on one occasion during the First World War my mother was outside near the horse and cart awaiting her meagre rations when she noticed Mrs Fielding taking a parcel from an upper shelf across to Nether Hall. It was obvious that the Freer family, known as gentry in those days, were getting preferential treatment. My mother was furious and threatened to report Mrs Fielding if it continued. Surely, she said, if there was any extra going it should go to my father and other workers in the foundry for working and sweating day and night for the war effort.

Soon after the outbreak of World War Two, when the Home Guard was formed a platoon was formed at Keyham. This belonged to what was known as C Company 6th Quorn Regiment of Leicestershire Home Guard. This platoon was very active. Its headquarters were in Keyham village hall. It was known in the early days as the Local Defence Volunteers or Look, Duck and Dodgem. All we had to identify us was a khaki arm band and after a time we were equipped with khaki denims. Our Commander in Chief was Lieutenant Swan. He really put us through our paces.

The Keyham platoon included volunteers from Leicester, Scraptoft Lane and the rest from Keyham (about 30 to 40 in all). We would meet on a Sunday morning on parade and assemble outside the village hall to be drilled. We had no rifles or other weapons but were told that we would be supplied in due course. In the meantime we had twelve bore shotguns

Member of 'C' company 6th (Quorn) Battalion, Leicestershire Home Guard. In this photograph are: Eric Linney, Bob Elliott, Walter Moore, Horace Walker, Ray Scarborough, Billy Treadwell, Robert Harrison, Rowles Harrison, and Alec Thompson.

and some 410s. My brother was told to bring his .22 air rifle. Those with 12 bore shotguns were supplied with a single bore lead pellet and were told to empty out the old shot from the 12 bore cartridges and insert in its place the single lead ball. This proved very powerful and when tested at 30 yards would penetrate a 2 ins wooden plank.

After some months we were fitted out with real khaki Home Guard uniforms. Some fitted and some didn't. It was made clear that our main duty was to look out for enemy parachutists at night, and to do this we were supplied with an old empty furniture van. This was situated along one side of Ingarsby Road. It was quite small and provided just enough room for two. This was occupied during each night by two of us. I was partnered on duty with Sergeant King each Friday night. We would stay awake until about 12pm, keeping watch. We often heard German planes passing overhead. The peculiar sound of the engines made them easy to identify.

Three bombs were dropped in a field near Scraptoft Wood. I was outside with Sergeant King. We could plainly hear them whistling when they were released and we dived in the ditch. It is probable that the plane was lost and the bombs were released before the plane returned home.

We had an old camp bed which we took in turns to use for a two-hour kip. At this time we were equipped with rifles and a small amount of ammunition. We were visited sometimes during the night by Lieutenant Swan in his Bentley to make sure we did not go to sleep.

I remember one moonlit night, after a plane passed over we noticed a white patch in the distance about three fields away. We went to investigate, only to find to our relief that it was a big heap of lime.

We had a Lewis Gun which we had to take to pieces and thoroughly understand its working. Afterwards it was taken on the gun range and we were allowed each in turn to fire three separate shots and then a burst of three, such was the shortage of ammunition.

Again, at the Butts, we were taken by a bus to practise throwing live hand grenades. This did not appeal to everyone as some couldn't even throw a cricket ball. I remember one chap who was very nervous. When inside the brick pit enclosure with the instructor we were instructed to stand up, pull out the pin and throw the grenade as far as possible, watching where it dropped, and then quickly duck down. This chap threw the grenade: it hit the front wall and bounced back in the pit. The instructor dived over the side to get out as the grenade exploded. He was hit in the foot and lost half a shoe and his foot was slightly injured. The poor chap left inside the pit escaped without a scratch. After this things were tightened up.

We were, of course, supplied with the army-type gas mask and had to attend lectures in the village hall and learn all about mustard and phosgene gases, the two gases thought most likely to be used by the enemy.

I was living at Colchester Road during World War Two. I managed to use our firm's lorry to get to Keyham for my Friday night duty. This was parked at The White House until the morning. I would then return home and change from the Home Guard uniform, have my breakfast and be at work at Gough Road by 7.30am.

Life was pretty hectic. Fire watching occupied one other night in the week when a rota was formed at the works. Two of us were on duty each night.

At the beginning of the war three bombs were dropped on the factory next door to the foundry. This caused considerable damage but fortunately no casualties. Our works escaped with minor damage.

We had a small amount of damage to a large greenhouse which we had hoped to retain on part of the Gough Road site. We decided, in view of the possibility of further air raids, the greenhouse should be sold.

There was no doubt that our commanding officers took a very serious view of our training and we were taken on various manoeuvres at night as well as day. Our training was very thorough and we were confidentially informed that an invasion by the Germans was a distinct possibility. We were told if this should happen to bring as much food with us as possible. We were allowed to keep our rifles at home. I remember Lieutenant Lee saying 'If each of you kill at least one German the invasion cannot succeed'. I think after this that at least some of us realised the importance of the Home Guard and what might be expected of us.

I first met Muriel, my future wife, during the summer of 1936 but it was not until 1938 that our friendship developed.

During the early part of 1939 Muriel persuaded me to take her to meet her relations in Dorset. They lived in a small cottage in Corfe Castle village, where she was born. It was Easter and it fell late in that year. The weather was wonderful – continuous sunshine. I had an open red two-seater MG which my brother and I owned and shared and had purchased during 1936. This car was new and was on offer for £222 in a showroom on London Road. After much haggling it was reduced to £200 for cash. This was for many years our pride and joy and today is still in the family.

During our trip to Dorset, so good was the weather, we were able to have the hood down all the time, and dressed in ordinary jackets.

On our arrival I was introduced to Muriel's aunt and her grandmother who was 85. Arrangements were made for me to sleep at a lady's house a short distance away. I had a four poster bed with curtains, and there was a smell of lavender. I think this was one of my most enjoyable holidays and I cannot recollect an Easter either before or since when the weather was so good.

We were married in 1941 on July 19th. Being wartime it was difficult to find somewhere for the reception. However, a small gathering was arranged at a small restaurant in the High Street in Leicester. We were married at St. Mary's Church, Humberstone and after the service we were met outside the church with a guard of honour of fixed bayonets by the Keyham Home Guard.

We arranged to spend our week's honeymoon in a boarding house at Blackpool recommended by a friend. We saved up just enough petrol to take us there and back with the MG but we dared not use it during the time we were there. We were made very comfortable and we were told that Blackpool was practically taken over by the RAF. After we had just retired to bed there was an air raid warning. I think after our journey and the events of the day, we were too tired to let this worry us.

A month before our marriage I was looking out for somewhere to live to start our married life. We decided to buy a detached house in Colchester Road. It had three bedrooms with a garage and a very small plot of land at the front and rear. The price was £650. We would be the second owners from new. I felt this would be a convenient place to live. No petrol was available during the war for our MG car. I used Muriel's cycle to get backwards and forwards to work and was able to come home for lunch at mid-day on occasions.

My father had been talking of retiring. I therefore had in mind perhaps some time after the war to return to Keyham and take over the family house.

We stayed at Colchester Road for 6½ years during which time two of our children were born.

Muriel in the MG, 1939.

David, the eldest, was born in June 1942. Arrangements were made for Muriel to have her confinement at a nursing home in Clarendon Park Road but staying with her mother and father in Haynes Road before the expected event.

Maureen came next in January 1945. A similar arrangement was made for Maureen, but this time the nursing home was The Laurels in Uppingham Road. It so happened that Maureen was born a week or two early. I was not altogether unprepared and had arranged for a taxi man who lived opposite to be available should he be required during the night. I rang the doctor from a local call box and was advised to get Muriel to the nursing home as soon as possible. I rang and knocked on the door of the taxi driver but to no avail. He would not get up. We decided, therefore, to catch the first workmen's bus which went by at 6am. It had been snowing during the night and the road was covered with ice. We waited a short time at the bus stop and when it arrived I explained to the conductor the position. He called out to the driver 'Step on it George – we've got a maternity case on board'.

During the war I dug up our small lawn at the rear of the house and planted it with potatoes, such was the shortage of vegetables. After the war I extended the rear of the garage to form a wash-house as the kitchen accommodation was very small.

Having a modern foundry in the town, with the conveniences of good electricity, gas and water supplies and a tall chimney where we were able to exhaust the fumes from the furnaces, Robert and I felt that we were now in a good position to compete.

Soon after the war started our core makers were called up for National Service. Core makers were not considered to be in a reserved occupation although they were an essential part of running a foundry. We were told by the Ministry of Supply that we should employ women. This meant an extension had to be built, separated from the main foundry. This was quickly built and fitted out for women workers. A suitable core drying oven was installed. Two local women were engaged. They were followed by my sister Mavis, who lived nearby, and my brother's wife, Norma. They were found to be very adept and proved very satisfactory although large heavy cores still had to be made in the foundry by men moulders.

It was the summer of 1945. At last the war was over, and gradually restrictions were lifted and we were able to resume the making of castings for commercial use. There was a distinct shortage of work for some time while engineering firms re-tooled to resume their normal products. Eventually we became quite busy supplying our customers who were receiving orders to replace the many shortages caused by the war.

During the next three or four years, due to the increase in orders, it became obvious that we needed to have more room and it was time to extend. I had been able to acquire some land from the allotment holders adjoining our premises. I spent quite some time over the years visiting them in the evenings and weekends explaining that I needed the land for extensions. Some agreed to sell. Gradually I obtained the land that I needed for a sizeable extension. In one case the client had lost his deeds and I had to take the risk of completion without deeds. On another occasion a near neighbour with a small engineering works bought a plot which would have impeded any future extension. He could not be persuaded to sell, and was already established on the other side of Gough Road but badly needed more room. I found out that land was available next to his small factory. I was able to purchase this and was now in a bargaining position. He was very surprised when I offered him land next to his building in exchange for the plot that we needed. A deal was eventually completed.

The new extension gradually got under way. There were many difficulties to overcome. The builder was short of labour and it was difficult to obtain the necessary licence for the steel that was needed for crane extensions and runways. It was a question of priorities and we were low on the list.

I decided that the two bays that we needed would be 30 feet wide and approximately 90 feet long. These should run at right angles to the existing building. This proved to be the right decision and the cranes were able to run the whole length of the new extension and beyond if further extensions were planned.

My father came over to look at this further commitment of which I think he approved.

It was at this stage that my brother and I were appointed joint managing directors of the Company.

We settled down at Gough Road in the new foundry. Our staff increased to about twenty by the end of 1941. I think they were pleased with their new environment.

It was about this time that it was decided that the business be formed into a Limited Liability company. This was incorporated and became known as R.C. Harrison & Sons Ltd with a capital of £5000. My brother and I were made Directors. My sister, Marjorie, was Secretary. The shareholdings were as follows:

R.C. Harrison – Managing Director	3900 £1 shares
E.R. Harrison – Director	500 £1 shares
J.C.R. Harrison – Director	500 £1 shares
M.A. Harrison – Secretary	100 £1 shares

After moving the foundry from Keyham in 1939 to the new foundry at Gough Road, Leicester, the old foundry buildings at Keyham were more or less in a derelict state. Knowing we were going to move as soon as possible the maintenance had been neglected.

My father and Alice were on their own. My brother Robert was married two months before me. My sister Mavis was also married. When my sisters had all left home, my father decided to retire. He bought in 1947 a bungalow with a large garden at Countesthorpe. He would hire a car to take him to the foundry once or twice a week.

My father paid regular visits to the foundry until approximately six months before his death. His health then was beginning to fail and he died during November 1949 at the age of 75. Robert and I were with him when he died.

Alice stayed on at Countesthorpe in the bungalow for some months and then decided to move down to All Hallows in Kent to live with her daughter Mildred and son-in-law John.

So it was during 1947 that I decided to buy the family house from my father and with my family come back to live at Keyham. Much remained to be done both inside the house and out. We had central heating installed, a new bathroom and lots of other improvements including the removal of ceilings which revealed old oak beams.

Outside, the old foundry was pulled down and the bricks used to form a south boundary wall. The En Tout Cas Company were engaged to landscape the garden after removal of the foundry residue. This was bull-dozed down to a lower level and made flat and then completely covered with a foot of new soil taken from one half of the paddock. This operation took between six and eight weeks including building the retaining walls, paved areas, pergolas and a turfed lawn.

On the south wall we planted espalier fruit trees, peaches, nectarines and fig plus a climbing passion flower. These were all successful and we

The new foundry at Gough Road, Leicester, 1939.

Interior of the Gough Rd Foundry in 1948.

Demolition of the foundry at the rear of the White House, 1948. It stood to the right of the picture.

The garden at the rear of the White House after completion of landscaping.

had lots of ripe fruit. The rich soil removed from the paddock provided us with an excellent kitchen garden. I can recall harvesting peas and carrots at the beginning of June.

The MG car that my brother and I owned was used by each of us on alternate weekends. Robert was keen on dancing and often went to the Palais de Dance in the Haymarket, Leicester, leaving the MG on the open car park nearby. On three occasions it was stolen by someone, probably to get a free ride home. I would get a phone call about 12pm while in bed. 'Will you come and pick me up, the MG has been stolen.' I would get out of bed not feeling very pleased and collect him in my father's second-hand Triumph Gloria car. The ignition key in an MG in those days was no more than a flat piece of steel which anyone could make or obtain. The car was found by the police undamaged the next day.

The same thing happened for a second time a month or two later. I was again called out at midnight. The car again was found the next day undamaged.

I was getting tired of being fetched out of bed so I said that if it happened again he could walk home. However, it did happen for a third time and it was in the winter. In spite of the removal of the rotor arm, someone armed themselves with one of these, easily obtainable from an MG garage. It was past midnight and I looked out of the window – a raging snowstorm was in progress and I relented and once more got out the car to collect him. The car on this occasion was not found until several weeks had passed. It had been run into a ditch well back off the road and was so well covered with drifting snow that it was invisible. It was found somewhere near Market Harborough, when the snow had melted. The cylinder head was cracked, also the engine block and the radiator. The car was fully insured by the Prudential Insurance Company.

My father never took to driving any other car than the Model T Ford. When this model became obsolete with its all-foot controls he gave up driving. I used the Triumph for business purposes and took my father and Alice to the Opera House. This was something they both enjoyed. I also took them to Grays in Essex to Alice's old home.

During 1937 I decided I would pursue my hobby of amateur radio and build myself a radio shack, with the help of friends, in the paddock well away from everybody. I had used a small bedroom in the house for my earlier experiments.

The Leicester Corporation had already started the demolition of the Causeway Lane properties. An old factory near to the foundry was being pulled down. This was just opposite where I was working and I was authorised to take what I wanted using my father's lorry. After work I loaded it up with bricks and stone sills. Two public houses were included in the demolition scheme and I was able to obtain some nice glazed shaped bricks which I used for the fireplace.

It was a slow job as I had no building experience. I remember digging out the foundations at midnight during one frosty beautiful moonlit night.

Building the radio
shack.

I had to have the windows made, but apart from this everything else was second-hand. I should have said that planning permission had to be obtained from Billesdon Council and the plans drawn by an architect. The building was approximately 14 ft square outside, made of brick with a slated roof. The floor was well spaced from the ground, the stone sills I acquired being used for steps leading up to the door.

At this stage I decided to apply to the Post Office for an experimental licence. This was known as an A.A. Licence (Artificial Aerial) which if granted would enable me to use a transmitter, but not connected to an aerial, and therefore I could not cause any outside interference. The idea of this was to enable me to acquire knowledge of transmitting. The licence arrived in due course with my call sign 2 D G A. This was during 1938. I was now authorised to carry out experiments ready for the time when I might be granted a whole B Licence.

It was now time to consider a support for an aerial. A mast was out of the question at this stage. I acquired some lengths of 2¼ ins diameter heavy steel steam pipe. These were securely screwed together forming a 55 ft length. A 15 ft heavy duty post or derrick was used with a pulley at the top. This derrick was securely guyed for the initial lift. A cable over a pulley on the top of the derrick was positioned near the centre of the pipe, then a hand operated winch was used. Support posts to hold the guy wires were firmly positioned in the ground. After much work and planning the moment came to erect it vertically. The guy cables were laid out on the ground and with the help of half a dozen or so villagers the lift began. The base of the pipe was secured on a slab in a shallow hole and when the winding began on the winch it began to rise, bending and

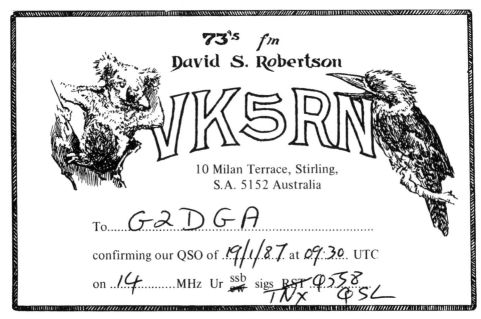

Confirmation card of two-way communication from Stirling, nr Perth, Australia.

The Radio shack and
Aerial mast.

swaying alarmingly side to side. Steadily it rose a bit, the men on the guy ropes taking the tension as it became nearly vertical. The guy ropes were quickly attached to the mooring posts and everything made fast and safe.

The building of the radio shack was completed in 1939. It was then that I received a visit from a General Post Office Official. My experimental transmitting equipment was to be confiscated. This applied to all radio amateurs for the duration of the war. It was safely returned to me when the war was over. It was by then of course completely out of date.

My early experiments and knowledge of amateur radio stood me in good stead and I was often called in when someone's radio set went wrong. They were all battery operated in those days. The usual faults were worn-out dry batteries or accumulators that needed charging. I would arrange for my father to drop them off at Scraptoft to a Mr Culpin who had a battery charging set.

I had let my experimental licence lapse. This was a mistake. I should have renewed it each year. However, I had to forget about transmitting. I kept in touch listening on my home made short wave receiver and was able to listen to the American Radio Amateurs. They were building and acquiring steel towers with revolving beams on top. I decided that this was something I would like to acquire in the future.

It was not until 1979 that I made up my mind to make a determined effort to qualify and become a licensed radio amateur Class B. To do this I had to take a City and Guilds Radio Amateur Examination. The courses were held at Charles Keene College, Leicester, and consisted of three hours from six until nine at night on one night a week. I must admit that sometimes after a hard day in the foundry I started to nod off near nine o'clock. It was like going back to school. After failing the exam the first time I had to try a second thus taking the course over again. This time I was successful and was awarded a coveted City and Guilds Certificate Grade B. My call sign was G8WDH. I was now permitted to transmit on the air but restricted to certain very high frequency wave bands. To become a full-blown radio amateur and to be awarded an A licence it was necessary to pass a Morse Code test. This consisted of receiving and transmitting at 12 words a minute for three minutes each and being allowed two errors.

I had to decide whether to go the whole way. My family encouraged me and one of my daughters bought me a set of practice Morse records. These were a great help, but even so it took me many months of continued practice and more practice and still I was not happy that I was ready to take the test.

My wife finally persuaded me to have a go. An appointment was made at the Post Office Wireless Station at Trusthorpe near Cleethorpes. This was one morning at 9am. I was the first of several to take the test that day. Muriel and I decided to travel to Cleethorpes the night before. We stayed at a small hotel nearby. We got up early in the morning and had a brisk walk along the sea front arriving for the test prompt at 9am. The examiner did all he could to make me feel at ease. I donned a pair of headphones and with my finger on the Morse key the test commenced.

I think the six minutes were the longest in my life and it was a great thrill to be told that I had passed. I know I made two or three mistakes but perhaps the examiner took pity on me because of my age. I was 73. The Radio Amateur Morse Code Exam is no longer carried out at the Post Office Wireless Stations but has been taken over by the Radio Society of Great Britain. The post office station at Trusthorpe now operates on a completely automatic system – no operators are required. I hope my description of becoming a radio amateur will not give you the impression that it is a difficult task. It is not if you are willing to practise and practise and of course don't leave it until you are seventy three!

Eighteen months after returning to The White House we had an increase in our family. On October 25th 1949 Muriel gave birth to twins at the Fielding Johnson Hospital which was then a private hospital in Regents Road, Leicester.

The birth of twins was a complete surprise as only one baby was expected. We named them Robert and Julia and they were christened in Keyham Church.

My father saw them only once, as he died the following month.

My father's marriage to Alice proved her to be a very capable person and a good housekeeper. We were all well looked after. Her daughter Mildred lived with her elderly grandparents at Grays in Essex. When her mother married my father she came to live with us after she had finished her schooling. Mildred settled down at The White House and became one of the family, getting on well with my sisters.

After leaving school each of my sisters started work at the age of 14. They all later married.

My eldest sister Cissie, afterwards known as Cicely, travelled around to different parts of the world but finally settled down and married Frederic de Harvas who ran a school for backward children in the county of Surrey.

My sister Mavis married Robert Gundle, who was in the Air Force. After the war he rejoined his father's engineering business in Leicester where they manufactured scales. He was made a Director. They had two daughters.

My sister Ethelwynne, afterwards known as Anne, married a Captain in the Air Force, John Carrington. After the war he took up commercial flying joining Cathay Pacific Airlines in Hong Kong where he and my sister lived for nearly twenty years. He became Chief Pilot and with my sister stayed there until his retirement. They had one son, John. After retirement they went to live in Ireland for a few years and then to the Dordogne Valley in France.

My youngest sister Marjorie married Tony Graham, who was also in the Armed Forces. When he was demobbed he joined his father's sack manufacturing business in Luton. Marjorie and Tony had two sons and two daughters.

My step-sister Mildred married a farmer, John Williams. They bought West End Farm, Keyham, and they farmed it for a short time. They sold the farm to the Fowler family and they then moved to All Hallows in Kent where they became tenants of the local inn.

Looking back in the past many changes have taken place in the fields around Keyham.

Brick buildings with slated roofs were needed in the winter months to provide shelter for livestock, horses, calf places, etc. and the storage of hay. No doubt they were also useful to give shelter to farm workers in the fields during very bad weather, incidentally providing sleeping accommodation for tramps during the summer months.

Old Crommy, a man of the roads, occupied one of these buildings during the summer. Crommy had a large bushy beard and as children we were told not to go near the buildings where he slept.

However, he was quite harmless and it was said he had seen better days. He would sit about under hedges at the road side partly concealed and people would often get a start coming across him unexpectedly.

In days gone by I have spent very many happy hours in the fields and the woods and spinneys and around the brook near Keyham. I used to think what a pity to see these buildings gradually deteriorate over the years. Over many years all the buildings have disappeared – victims to the weather and neglect, until only a heap of bricks remained. These were then carried away gradually to the nearest gateway to provide hardcore leaving no trace of what was once a substantial brick building.

Farming methods have changed over the years. Arable farming which is less labour-intensive has taken the place of the breeding of livestock and dairy farming, so the buildings were no longer required. Birds missed them most of all. They proved ideal nesting sites for barn owls, swallows and others to rear their young.

It was decided during 1936 that there were enough young men in the village to start a cricket club. We had no difficulty in getting permission from Mr H.T. Hincks to use the cricket pitch. This was the ground that was previously used by the Baxter team during 1922.

The first snag we encountered was that we were unable to find the metal sockets used for the fencing. They had apparently sunk into the ground since they were last used. I set to work having six wooden formers made to provide concrete sockets, these to take the six 5 by 4 ins. wooden posts required to take two strands of barbed wire to form a cattleproof fence.

On the day of a match, usually a Saturday, the posts would be lifted out beyond the outfield. I remember spending all my Easter holidays attending to this. Having the firm's lorry I was able to take the necessary materials to the site. With the help of others we completed the job. Our first match was during May. Mr Hincks' cow man kindly had the cattle taken out of the field during match days.

Mr Eric Fielding and his brother the late Mr Charles Fielding, who farmed at Glebe Farm, were regular players and members of the club. Eric was match secretary and always managed to get a full fixture list for the season including night matches and an all day match with Norton and Gaulby on Whit Monday. Eric kept wicket for the club and was quite successful. Many enjoyable matches were played.

Unfortunately the war during 1939 put a stop to our activities. It was not until 1951 that we got going again. This was by joining Quenby Cricket Club, whose ground was adjoining Quenby Park. It was decided to put down a concrete and matting wicket. This was because of the difficulty of finding a groundsman. Sir Harold Nutting was President with Sir George Earle, Lieutenant Colonel Gemmel, A.T. Sharp, Mrs Kirkpatrick and others as Vice Presidents. Their generous annual donations were collected by our able secretary, Mr H. Austick, who visited their respective homes.

The overlaid matting on concrete had one advantage: it was very rare for the weather to interfere with play. Our visiting opponents were not altogether happy on our wicket except when they were winning. Owing to the extra bounce of the ball many good balls which would have normally hit the wicket went over the top. However, we had no difficulty in getting fixtures.

Lord Hungarton was a Chairman of the Club and a regular onlooker to our home matches. Also Anthony Nutting MP, who on rare occasions played for the Club.

After my return to the family house at Keyham in 1948 with my wife and family I would have been content to settle down and spend the rest of my life at Keyham. But events proved otherwise.

It happened one day in 1962 that Maureen was browsing through the *Leicester Graphic* and remarked 'Look at this lovely house for sale'. My wife had a look and eventually I was persuaded to take notice. This was followed by an appointment for us to have a look round.

It was a beautiful big house in Oadby called Hall Leys, approached by a long private drive. There were three acres of lawns and gardens. Maureen said 'Wouldn't it be wonderful to live there.' I decided to have a few words with the agents and they convinced me that Hall Leys was all it was made out to be.

I discovered that I knew the gardener who had worked there for a number of years and who was now retired. He had been the head gardener for Corahs who lived at Scraptoft Hall and I had played cricket with his two sons. I decided that I would look him up. He dispelled any fears I might have had but he said I would need a full-time gardener.

I decided I had all the information I required and the best thing I could do was to forget all about it. It was two weeks to the sale, which was by auction. I had almost forgotten the date. I was working at the foundry on the date of the auction sale and without giving it a thought when David, my eldest son, came to where I was working and said 'Dad, aren't you going to that sale – Mum will be disappointed when you get home and tell her you haven't attended it'. He said, 'Come on, put on your coat and I will run you there'. I thought, well, maybe I had better attend. I put on my coat and was quickly driven there. There were two houses for sale by auction. The first house seemed to attract quite a lot of attention. There was brisk bidding and it was soon sold.

Now the auctioneer started to describe Hall Leys, concentrating on all its features and merits. The bidding started, I believe, at £5,000. There were three or four people bidding one after another. It reached the price of £10,000 and the bidding stopped and I thought now was my chance. I heard the auctioneer say to his clerk 'There's Mr Harrison at the back over there'. I started bidding which was quickly taken up in £500 bids by one person. I made a second bid which was followed by a third.

This was quickly equalled and I could see that this other gentleman intended to buy it, and so it proved. I gave a little sigh of relief, glad I could say that I had attended the sale. When I got home, my wife and family were disappointed at the news and remarked, 'Why didn't you bid a bit more, you might have been lucky'.

Two days later I had a telephone call from the estate agents asking whether I was still interested in Hall Leys. I replied, 'What's happened and what is the matter with it?' They replied, 'Nothing – Mr so and so, a well known Leicester businessman has decided he does not want it, and as you were the next highest bidder we are offering it to you.' My remark to this was 'How much less do you think he will accept?' They replied 'I don't suppose he will want to take much less.' I then offered £100 less than his bid. The next day this was accepted, and I became the owner of Hall Leys.

I did not break the news to my family until it was confirmed. When I did, imagine their surprise and delight and how they were dancing around me with joy. We sold The White House and moved to Hall Leys where we spent 12½ happy years.

During the time we were living at Hall Leys, our daughter Julia was married at Oadby Church to Mr Derek Hodson. This was in August 1972. The large lawn in front of the house was an ideal place for a marquee to be erected. This was arranged and it was large enough to accommodate over one hundred guests. Our gardener, Mr Roy Spark, decorated it beautifully with roses and other flowers and he also made the bouquets for the bride and bridesmaids.

Three weeks later, Julia's twin brother, Robert, was married to Josephine Meadows. The wedding was held at Smeeton Westerby and their reception was held at a local hotel. We have happy memories of both occasions. Over the years Julia and Derek had three children, 2 daughters and a son. Robert and Jo had a son and daughter.

As my family grew up I was able to relive the pleasures of my youth in the fields and spinneys; I took them for walks in the fields showing them where to bird-watch and look for birds' nests. One day, when they were about four, I took Robert and Julia to what they called the beetle tree, an old dead ash tree blown over in a gale. The tree, stripped of its bark with bare branches sticking out from the trunk, looked like a beetle. The trunk was hollow from the base to the top. It was about 15 to 20 feet from the ground to the top. Birds would enter to build their nests, sometimes a tawny owl or a jackdaw. There was a large hole in the lower half of the trunk about six feet from the ground. The twins stood near this waiting for me while I climbed up the trunk to see if there was a nest. Astride I worked myself up to the top of the trunk bit by bit. I was about half way along when I heard a rustling sound. Looking back I saw a fox come out of the hole landing at the twin's feet. Within a second or two a second one jumped out scampering off down the field. Julia called out 'send another one down Dad'. I climbed down from the tree-top a little disappointed as I hadn't been able to find a nest as I usually did.

We continued down the fields to the brook where kingfishers used to breed. Among the reeds a reed bunting's nest could be found.

Above the reed bed on the wet and boggy bank clumps of marsh marigolds never failed to appear during the spring. On the bank above was a badger's sett. This sett was at one time regularly occupied but for some years now has been deserted.

This delightful spot, about one acre in extent, known as The Miles Piece, was given to the Leicester and Rutland Wild Life Trust for Nature Conservation by the late Mrs I. Cheales of Nether Hall, Keyham.

Mr and Mrs Cheales lived in South Africa for many years before coming to live in Lincolnshire where Mr Cheales was to manage a farm. While there they made occasional visits to Keyham. Mr Cheales was a keen cricketer and played regularly for Skegness Town. During his visits to Keyham he would join in and play for the village cricket team.

At this time the Hirst family occupied the Nether Hall having recently moved from the Manor House at Beeby. The Hall was still owned by the Miles family and while the Hirst family occupied it they allowed the grounds to be used in 1935 for a garden fete. This was to raise money for

The author on the fallen ash tree with the twins, a fox leaving the base of the tree, soon to be followed by a second one. Julia is shouting 'send another one down, Dad!'

Mrs I. Cheales, daughter of the late Mr W.F. Miles of Nether Hall, Keyham, 1969.

funds for the upkeep of the church and also provide funds for the cricket club.

Mr Hirst was a hoisery manufacturer and had four sons and two daughters, Peggy and Mary. Their sons were Tom, Peter, Oswald and Francis. Oswald was killed during World War Two. They stayed in the village until 1944.

After Mr Cheales decided to retire in 1945, he and his wife came to live at Keyham at the Nether Hall. They gave permission for the use of the lawn in front of their house for the village fete. This became a yearly event. The proceeds were distributed between the Church and the Village Hall. The late Mr Harry Austick, as Chairman, was prominent in organising the events. A children's fancy dress parade was always staged along with many side shows. A dance was held in the evening in the village hall. The fetes were opened by prominent local people, introduced by the Vicar of that time.

The Quorn hounds were invited to meet on their lawn once a year, while the rest of the hunt assembled in their adjoining field known as the Bullock Field.

Mrs Cheales was very active in the village and became the village representative on the Billesdon Council. The villagers had a surprise one day when a bulldozer appeared down Snows Lane and started ripping up the hedge bordering the lane and Mr Fowler's field. This was the start of the development of the eleven houses that were built in 1963. No one in the village had any indication that this was going to take place. It can be said, however, that the addition to the village has proved an asset and many of the new inhabitants have taken a keen interest in its welfare.

Mr Bill Lester, the foundry manager at Causeway Lane for many years, who now lived at the top of the village, was asked to umpire for Keyham Cricket Club. It was an evening match. Mr Lester had often acted as umpire for league cricket in his younger days. Unfortunately on this occasion he met with a serious accident whilst umpiring. His leg was broken by a very low travelling ball hit by the opposite batsman. The match was cancelled and the ambulance sent for. He was conveyed to the Leicester Royal Infirmary where I am pleased to say he made a complete recovery.

The players of the cricket match got together to raise a subscription for the benefit of Mr Lester. This was followed by a further cricket match and a dance in the Keyham Village Hall to further increase the funds.

It may be remembered that when my father acquired land to build bungalows for his men during 1920, the land was in the Scraptoft parish and this surplus land was let for several years to a local farmer.

It was during the later twenties. Mr Fielding Johnson, a very well known local businessman and benefactor, was farming in the Beeby and Scraptoft and Keyham areas. My father sold him the spare land he no longer required. Mr Fielding Johnson owned many acres of land and farms in the area including farm cottages and buildings. He had a tall wooden silo built for storing silage. This was reinforced on the outside with iron bands. Mr Fielding Johnson may have been the first farmer in Leicestershire to feed silage to his cattle. The tall wooden silo was quite an innovation in those days and a landmark for many years.

He did much to improve the property and the land. One way was the

Garden fete at Nether Hall, Snow's Lane, Keyham, 1950.

use of basic slag as a fertiliser. This was good for the land but put paid to some of the best mushroom fields.

After the death of Mr Fielding Johnson in 1932 his executors sold his 1666 acres of land. The 14-acre piece of land came on the market again some years later and was bought by my brother Robert. He and his wife Norma and son Peter lived on the outskirts of the east side of Leicester. Robert was born at Keyham and was very fond of the countryside.

The 14 acres of land he now owned was surrounded by fields; it sloped down to the south and so was protected from the north winds. A brook with high banks ran across the lower part of the field. In the roots of a large ash tree growing at the side of the brook was a badger's sett.

A bridge of sleepers was put over the stream and the other side was fully planted with trees. Half way down the field a clear spring flowed. This spring had never been known to run dry. A watercress bed was formed just below. With the help of a retired friend, called Leslie, much tree planting was done, including a large fruit orchard of apples, pears, plums, and a double row of standard dessert cherry trees.

This was not a commercial enterprise. It was my brother's hobby and relaxation. It was, however, his hope that one day with his family he might live on the site. He applied for planning permission to build a stone house but his application was turned down by the planning authorities.

Robert became a member of The Men of Trees.

The death of Mr H.T. Hincks, at the end of 1939, was the end of an era for Keyham. During the time from 1919 until his death he farmed the whole of the Keyham estate. It was not until 1941 that the estate was split up and sold. There were five farms – about 700 acres in total.

The Top Hall was sold to a Mr Black, a cinema owner in Leicester. The five farms were each sold separately, some to Mr Aubrey Sharp as a speculative venture (they were sold again soon afterwards). Mr Sharp later acquired the Top Hall from Mr Black, but rented it to the Allan family.

Mr Aubrey Sharp in his young days was a well known Leicestershire County Cricketer and played for Leicester. He lived at the Nether Hall, Scraptoft.

Some time after the Top Hall was sold Miss Kitty Hincks left the village to live in Kent. Miss Emily Hincks stayed on in the village for a short time going to live at the house now known as The Fold. It was later sold to three maiden ladies; Miss Graydon, Miss Antrobus and Miss Moore. The three ladies took over The Fold as a restaurant (booking only). There was a large garden and orchard adjoining The Fold. This was cultivated as a vegetable garden by Miss Moore. The cooking was undertaken by Miss Antrobus while Miss Graydon served at table. They carried on their business for a number of years. The Fold is now a private house.

After The Fold was sold Miss Emily Hincks left the village. Before leaving she sold bottles of vintage port wine for £1 each. This was only for the village people and only one at a time. Maybe this was part of the Squire's wine cellar.

The Post Office was sold to Miss Healey, as sitting tenant; she occupied it for more than 40 years.

The Dog and Gun Public House became the property of Messrs Everards Brewery. Mr Colin Dowsett became the landlord in 1962 and stayed for 30 years until retirement.

The remaining cottages were sold privately by Miss Kitty Hincks. These were the cottages situated between the Old School and the Pub.

The farm known as West End Farm and The White House were not part of the Miles inheritance, so they were not disturbed during the reign of Mr H.T. Hincks. The house and paddocks known as Cottage Farm were also sold privately. The new owners of the farms stayed for many years; milk from some was sold in the village. As time went on Government restrictions were imposed on small dairy farms. The high cost of complying with these restrictions made it difficult for them to continue. One by one the four farmers moved, some to retire and some to take on farms elsewhere. The farmhouses were retained and sold separately to become private residences.

There was one exception however. The occupants of The White House Farm stayed in the village of Keyham but moved house to an agricultural cottage at the far end of the village, retaining their land. Keyham can say, therefore, that it still has a farm in the village. Some of the land of these farms was sold to Kirby & West.

When the farmhouses became vacant they were sold and modernised, and the barns were converted into houses and are occupied by business and professional people.

The Allan family, who stayed at the Top Hall for some years, kept bees in the paddock behind the Church. When the Allans left the village Mr Allan offered to give me the three hives of bees with all the accessories. I knew nothing whatever about keeping bees, but thought it an opportunity. The bees were free, provided I removed them within a few days. The family had bought a house at Thurnby.

It was winter time and there was four inches of snow on the ground. I was told that you must never move bees in the winter, but I had no choice. I was able to run my car close up to the hives and one by one they were loaded into the boot and transferred to their new site in my paddock about 200 or 300 yards away.

The bees showed signs of activity collecting pollen in the early spring. I bought a good book on beekeeping and took advice from a friend. When I moved to Oadby, the bees stayed in the paddock at Keyham. One day I had an urgent phone call – a complaint from the Landlord of the local pub, the Dog and Gun. He said there was a swarm of bees in the men's toilets. Indeed, the bees had swarmed and found a hole in the wall of the men's toilets, and had found their way between the plywood ceiling and the flat roof. They had not been noticed for two days. The Landlord was very concerned and told me that I had to remove them before six o'clock when the pub opened.

I called at the foundry pattern shop for our carpenter, Bill Salter. He collected his tools and we returned to take down the ceiling. I was fully protected but Bill had only some netting over his face.

The ceiling came down without too much trouble; and the swarm was in one corner. I had a smoker ready to give them a small puff. I was then able to grasp them with both hands and lower them into a skep prepared on the floor. This was then covered over with a white cloth. I was very lucky in having secured the queen. Taking the skep outside a short distance away and turning it over on a board leaving a small space underneath enabled the rest of the bees to join the swarm.

Bill was then able to replace the ceiling. The bees were rehived in a spare hive during the evening. In that short time the bees had made some comb and were already filling it with honey.

During the next five or six years the bees multiplied and I was able to increase the number of hives to ten.

My radio shack in the paddock proved an ideal place for the extraction of the honey from the combs. After the family and friends had been supplied, not forgetting the Allan family, I was able to sell the remainder to Messrs Simpkin & James for 3/6d per pound.

It was during 1958 that my youngest son Brian was born at The White House.

After the War when the school was no longer required for educational purposes, it remained empty for some months. When it was advertised for sale, I decided to make an offer which was accepted by the education authorities.

I thus became the owner of Keyham School. There was little interest in old properties in those days and it was used by the foundry for storing patterns for several years.

I had in mind that one day it might be converted into a house and perhaps be occupied by one of my sons.

David, my eldest son, was married in 1965. The old school was converted to a house and David and his wife Veronica moved in. During their time at the school they produced a family of four – three girls and a boy. They remained in the old school for fourteen years.

Meanwhile we were still living at Hall Leys, Oadby. Our house was one of three leading off a private drive leading on to Stoughton Road, Oadby. We had nearly three acres of gardens beautifully laid out with a large kitchen garden, mature trees and flowering shrubs.

It came as a shock when in 1973 most of the adjacent property and land was being sold for building. We too were approached to see if we would sell. My answer was a definite no; we occupied one of the nicest houses in Leicester. But we were told that the development of the estate would proceed whether we sold or not. If this happened we would find ourselves surrounded by many houses on two sides. We would also lose the private drive.

We gave very careful thought to the situation and finally decided to sell.

We had nine months to move. My thoughts turned to Keyham where I already owned Cottage Farm, and the land at the rear. I applied for permission to build but this was turned down by Market Harborough planning department on the grounds that it was outside the confines of the village (despite the existence of the houses in Snows Lane). I lodged an appeal but this was turned down.

I now had to make a move as the nine months' notice would soon expire. I put the matter in the hands of an estate agent and it was not long before I was offered an old stone house in the village of Ayston, Rutland. This house was known as Hall Cottage and had been part of Ayston Hall. We purchased this and moved in December 1973 and stayed there for six and a half years.

During our six and a half years at Hall Cottage, we made many friends. Our house was next door to Ayston Hall where Mr Finch with his wife and two sons lived.

My daughter Maureen was married during the time we lived at Ayston, to Colin Harrington who lived at Shepshed, in May 1975. A large marquee was erected on the lawn in front of the house. The reception for

The board of directors in 1986. Left to right: Peter Harrison (Technical), Terry Lock (Financial), Robert Harrison (Joint Managing Director), the author, David Harrison (Joint Managing Director) Tony Sharp (Technical Director), Brian Harrison (Die Casting Division).

15 ft diameter aluminium wheel made for Dunlop's of Leicester at the Gough Road Factory; approximate weight 4 tons.

Visit of Institute of British Foundrymen with Directors and staff at Gough Road, *c.* 1970.

Office and main foundry of R. C. Harrison and Sons Ltd. Rowles Harrison (Member of the Institute of British Foundryman) was joint Managing Director with his brother Robert for nearly 40 years.

R. C. Harrison's in the 1990s, die casting and pattern shop

approximately ninety guests was held there. Mr Finch allowed the wedding party to walk to the church across his garden. Maureen and Colin settled in Cambridgeshire and had two daughters and a son.

After we had settled down at Ayston I was asked to become a church warden. Ayston Church was in need of funds for its upkeep. My family arranged a garden party on our lawn. David, my eldest son, provided some attractive and unusual sideshows and stalls. It was a beautiful summer's day and we had a good attendance, many coming from Uppingham. The sum of £300 was raised.

While we were living at Ayston my wife and I decided to have a trip to Badby Woods and Fawsley Park in Northamptonshire. These were favourite haunts visited by my mother in her young days. At the time the estate was owned by Sir Charles Knightly.

The Lantern House was part of the estate. It was our intention to photograph it with a view to having it painted by a friend of ours. In the evening when we arrived home my family was waiting for us: there was some very bad news. My brother Robert had died suddenly from a heart attack. He was tending his trees in his fields; Leslie was with him when he died. This was shocking news for his wife Norma and son Peter and for all of us.

Robert and I had worked together in the foundry for nearly fifty years and had been joint managing directors since 1941. Robert died during 1976 aged sixty six.

During 1979 David was looking out for somewhere with more room. The Old Rectory at Hungarton had come up for sale and David decided that this would suit him and his family. It was a spacious house with lots of garage space which would enable him to pursue his hobby of the restoration of veteran cars. This meant the Old School House had to be sold.

After careful thought we decided to move back to Keyham and buy the Old School House from David. It was with some reservations that we left Ayston. I think my wife would have preferred to stay.

During 1979 I retired from the Company. I had no hesitation in leaving the running of the Company to my two sons and their fellow directors, their very hard working staff and workers who had proven themselves to be very capable and loyal. At a Company meeting I decided to relinquish the office of Managing Director as from the 31st August 1979. It was decided that Mr D.R. Harrison and Mr R.C. Harrison be appointed Joint Managing Directors to take effect from the 1st September 1979. I continued as a Director of the Company also acting as Chairman of the Board.

Now that I was free to leave the running of the Company to others I decided to turn my attention to my hobby, amateur radio.

My radio shack was situated in the paddock which adjoined the garden of The Old School. All I needed was permission from the local authority to erect a mast to support the necessary aerials.

I had already acquired a forty foot fixed mast from a radio friend. This had a four foot walk around at the top. I was a bit dubious about climbing this myself but I had a friend who was keen on the idea and who said that he would climb and adjust the aerial.

With this in mind I applied to Market Harborough District Council for planning permission. My application was turned down on the grounds that the tower would become an intrusion into the conservation village of Keyham and be detrimental to the rural character and visual amenities of the locality. Undeterred, however, I decided to try again, this time for a telescopic, forty foot mast professionally built for radio amateurs. It would have two hand-operated winches, one to reduce the minimum height to 25 ft and one to lower the mast to the ground level to assist in the fixing of aerials. Again for the second time my application was turned down.

The Market Harborough District planning department were supported by a number of local residents of the village who said it would be an eyesore and could be seen from their bedroom windows. Some were also afraid I might cause interference to their televisions.

I decided to make further concessions and promised to motorise the up and down section of the mast and said I would lower the mast when not in use. I joined the nationally based Radio Amateur Emergency Network, Raynet, authorising my station to be available in times of emergency. I also obtained a letter of support from the Radio Society of Great Britain. With these further concessions I submitted them to the planning department

Stand at National Exhibition Centre, 1991.

and after a further visit to the site they relented and I was given planning permission for the mast for the duration of my life.

The policy of steady expansion at the foundry enabled us to keep pace with our customers' increased casting requirements and our policy of ploughing back profits to keep up to date with the latest plant. It was decided to provide our own pattern shop and woodworking department. We had space upstairs on the first floor. This was fitted out with the necessary pattern making machinery and proved an asset to the company.

Our extensions over the years gradually used up all the land on the foundry side of Gough Road. I was always on the look out for future expansion. This would have to be on the opposite side of Gough Road. A wholesale fruit and potato warehouse eventually came up for sale. I was able to purchase this property plus the land at the rear. This gave us access to Robinson Road. This much larger building enabled the pattern shop to be moved to the ground floor leaving more room for office extension on the first floor.

It was the recession in the early 1980s that created a serious set-back for the Company. It was found necessary to part with some of our staff. Orders became very scarce and in some cases discontinued altogether. The recession continued for two to three years. During this time a new process became available to the foundry trade; the new method of bonding sand. We took advantage of these processes by investing in the necessary machinery and putting it into use. We were now in a good position if and when any upturn came.

Presentation of cheque to Clarrie Timson on completion of 50 years service.

The cross, 10 ft high and candlesticks 7 feet high, which were commissioned for the newly restored High Altar at St Paul's Cathedral, London in 1958, a memorial to the men and women of the Commonwealth killed in two wars. Most of the bronze castings for the three ornaments were made at the Gough Rd foundry and beautifully finished by fine gilding with jewels and enamelling by Knights of Wellingborough, the ecclesiastical engineers.

David, after twenty eight years' service with the Company (during part of this time being joint managing director with Robert) decided to leave the Company as a result of joining a partnership in a plastic company.

Brian, my youngest son, after 13 years with the Company, resigned as he wanted to travel and see the world. This he did for three years.

Peter, my nephew, then became Joint Managing Director with Robert and they are now successfuly running the business.

At the Foundry Exhibition held at the NEC in Birmingham we decided to exhibit. We booked a stand and displayed a variety of non-ferrous castings, large and small. Our stand created much interest which resulted in making ourselves known over a larger area.

It was decided to retain the Registered Name of the Company as R.C. Harrison and Sons Limited, but in addition to have a trading name of Harrison Castings. An attractive design was formulated and displayed at the exhibition and afterwards in front of the office buildings in Gough Road.

After we gradually recovered from the recession the Company began to grow from strength to strength from that very small beginning by my father in 1911 at the rear of The White House at Keyham. The Company can now claim to be one of the four largest sand foundries in the country. It is still owned and run by the Harrison family.

Coat of arms, cast in lead by the author for Sir Harold Nutting of Quenby Hall, in 1930.